MASTER THE JAPANESE
HIRAGANA & KATAKANA

A Handwriting Practice Workbook

Perfect your calligraphy skills and dominate the Japanese kana

by Lang Workbooks

Important Legal Information:

This workbook is a labor of love. Accordingly, if you are a teacher, a student of Japanese, or homeschooling your children, *I grant you the non-commercial right to photocopy any part of this workbook for your own, or your students, personal use.*

All further rights are reserved © 2020.

ISBN: 9781658847230

Stroke Order

Stroke Progression
ヽ ラ ネ ネ

Example Word
ネバネバ

Nebaneba

Translation: Persistence / Sticky

Ne
"Ne" as in "Net"
IPA: /ne/

Clear large letters make it easy to recognize even the most detailed characters.

Trace and Practice

Detailed instructions provide you with a strong foundation to build up your handwriting and pronunciation skills.

Variations

ネ ネ ネ ネ ネ ネ

Dedicated sections are designed to imprint proper stroke technique unto your muscle memory.

Font variations with an emphasis on varying handwriting styles train your brain to recognize each character based on its specific stroke order.

As a bonus, at the end of this workbook you'll find extra empty training pages. Feel free to photocopy these pages as needed to extend the lifetime value of your workbook.

Hiragana Index

あ A Ipa: /a/ — Page 5	い I Ipa: /i/ — Page 6	う U Ipa: /ɯ/ — Page 7	え E Ipa: /e/ — Page 8	お O Ipa: /o/ — Page 9
か Ka Ipa: /ka/ — Page 10	き Ki Ipa: /ki/ — Page 11	く Ku Ipa: /kɯ/ — Page 12	け Ke Ipa: /ke/ — Page 13	こ Ko Ipa: /ko/ — Page 14
さ Sa Ipa: /sa/ — Page 15	し Shi Ipa: /ɕi/ — Page 16	す Su Ipa: /sɯ/ — Page 17	せ Se Ipa: /se/ — Page 18	そ So Ipa: /so/ — Page 19
た Ta Ipa: /ta/ — Page 20	ち Chi Ipa: /tɕi/ — Page 21	つ Tsu Ipa: /tsɯ/ — Page 22	て Te Ipa: /te/ — Page 23	と To Ipa: /to/ — Page 24
な Na Ipa: /na/ — Page 25	に Ni Ipa: /ɲi/ — Page 26	ぬ Nu Ipa: /nɯ/ — Page 27	ね Ne Ipa: /ne/ — Page 28	の No Ipa: /no/ — Page 29
は Ha Ipa: /ha/ or /ɰa/ — Page 30	ひ Hi Ipa: /çi/ — Page 31	ふ Fu Ipa: /ɸɯ/ — Page 32	へ He Ipa: /ha/ or /e/ — Page 33	ほ Ho Ipa: /ho/ — Page 34
ま Ma Ipa: /ma/ — Page 35	み Mi Ipa: /mi/ — Page 36	む Mu Ipa: /mɯ/ — Page 37	め Me Ipa: /me/ — Page 38	も Mo Ipa: /mo/ — Page 39
や Ya Ipa: /ja/ — Page 40		ゆ Yu Ipa: /jɯ/ — Page 41		よ Yo Ipa: /jo/ — Page 42
ら Ra Ipa: /ra/ — Page 43	り Ri Ipa: /ri/ — Page 44	る Ru Ipa: /rɯ/ — Page 45	れ Re Ipa: /re/ — Page 46	ろ Ro Ipa: /ro/ — Page 47
わ Wa Ipa: /ɰa/ — Page 48	を Wo Ipa: /o/ — Page 49	ん N Ipa: /N/ — Page 50	っ Sukuon — Page 51	**Bonus Training Pages** Pages 52 - 53

Hiragana Reference Charts

The Dakuten and the Handakuten Diacritics
Page 104

The Yōon Digraphs
106

Combining the Yōon Digraphs With the Dakuten and the Handakuten
Page 108

Extra Training Pages
Pages 109 - 116

Katakana Index

ア A Ipa: /a/ Page 54	イ I Ipa: /i/ Page 55	ウ U Ipa: /ɯ/ Page 56	エ E Ipa: /e/ Page 57	オ O Ipa: /o/ Page 58
カ Ka Ipa: /ka/ Page 59	キ Ki Ipa: /ki/ Page 60	ク Ku Ipa: /kɯ/ Page 61	ケ Ke Ipa: /ke/ Page 62	コ Ko Ipa: /ko/ Page 63
サ Sa Ipa: /sa/ Page 64	シ Shi Ipa: /ɕi/ Page 65	ス Su Ipa: /sɯ/ Page 66	セ Se Ipa: /se/ Page 67	ソ So Ipa: /so/ Page 68
タ Ta Ipa: /ta/ Page 69	チ Chi Ipa: /tɕi/ Page 70	ツ Tsu Ipa: /tsɯ/ Page 71	テ Te Ipa: /te/ Page 72	ト To Ipa: /to/ Page 73
ナ Na Ipa: /na/ Page 74	ニ Ni Ipa: /ɲi/ Page 75	ヌ Nu Ipa: /nɯ/ Page 76	ネ Ne Ipa: /ne/ Page 77	ノ No Ipa: /no/ Page 78
ハ Ha Ipa: /ha/ or /ɰa/ Page 79	ヒ Hi Ipa: /çi/ Page 80	フ Fu Ipa: /ɸɯ/ Page 81	ヘ He Ipa: /ha/ or /e/ Page 82	ホ Ho Ipa: /ho/ Page 83
マ Ma Ipa: /ma/ Page 84	ミ Mi Ipa: /mi/ Page 85	ム Mu Ipa: /mɯ/ Page 86	メ Me Ipa: /me/ Page 87	モ Mo Ipa: /mo/ Page 88
ヤ Ya Ipa: /ja/ Page 89		ユ Yu Ipa: /jɯ/ Page 90		ヨ Yo Ipa: /jo/ Page 91
ラ Ra Ipa: /ra/ Page 92	リ Ri Ipa: /ri/ Page 93	ル Ru Ipa: /rɯ/ Page 94	レ Re Ipa: /re/ Page 95	ロ Ro Ipa: /ro/ Page 96
ワ Wa Ipa: /ɰa/ Page 97	ヲ Wo Ipa: /o/ Page 98	ン N Ipa: /ɴ/ Page 99	ッ Sukuon Page 100	ー Chōonpu Page 101

Bonus Training Pages
Pages 102 - 103

Katakana Reference Charts

The Dakuten and the Handakuten Diacritics
Page 105

The Yōon Digraphs
107

Combining the Yōon Digraphs With the Dakuten and the Handakuten
Page 108

Extra Training Pages
Pages 109 - 116

あ

A

"A" as in "f<u>a</u>ther"

IPA: /a/

Stroke Order

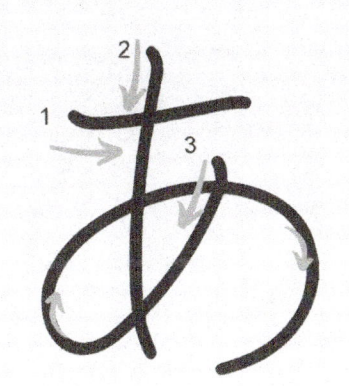

Stroke Progression

一 十 あ

Example Word

あさめし

Asameshi

Translation: Breakfast

Trace and Practice

Variations

あ あ あ あ あ あ

い

"Ee" as in "see"
IPA: /i/

Stroke Order

Stroke Progression
い い

Example Word
いちがつ
Ichigatsu

Translation: January

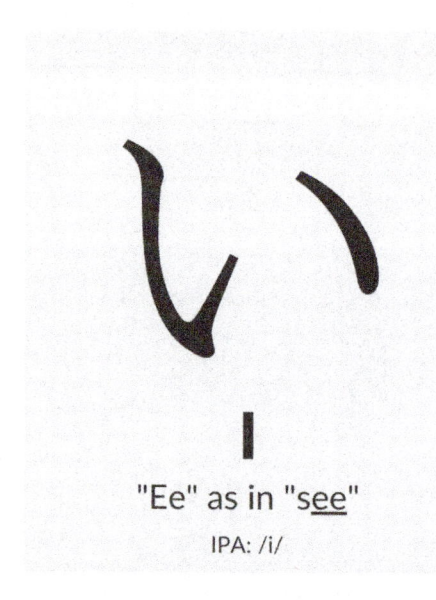

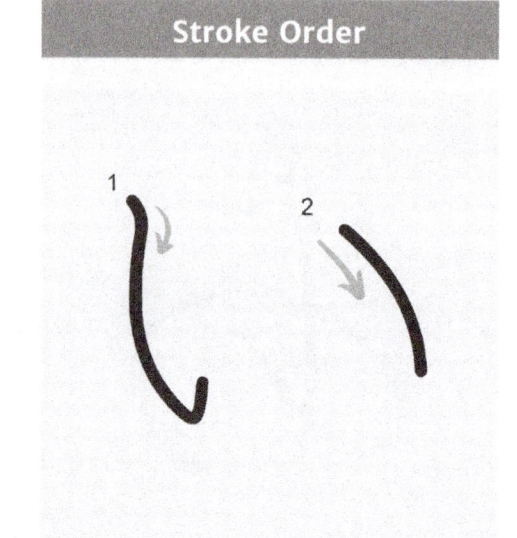

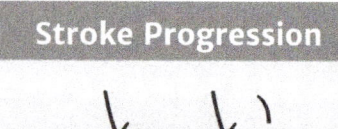

Trace and Practice

Variations

う

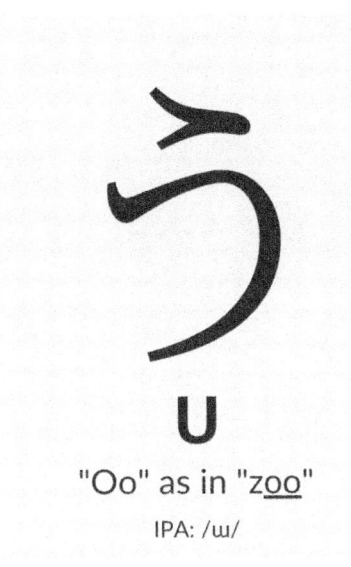

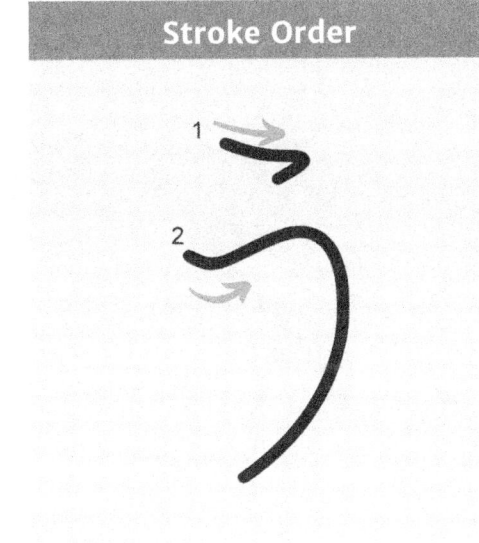

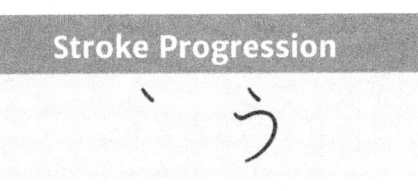

U

"Oo" as in "z<u>oo</u>"

IPA: /ɯ/

Stroke Order

Stroke Progression

Example Word

うれしい

Ureshī

Translation: Happy

Trace and Practice

Variations

うううう う

え

E

"E" as in "s**e**t"

IPA: /e/

Stroke Order

Stroke Progression

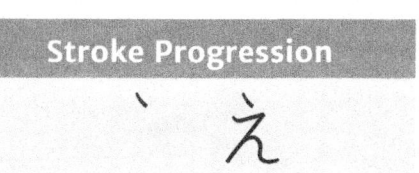

`え

Example Word

えんぴつ

Enpitsu

Translation: Pencil

Trace and Practice

Variations

お

"O" as in "B<u>o</u>at"
IPA: /o/

Stroke Order

Stroke Progression
　ー　お　お

Example Word
おふくろ
Ofukuro

Translation: Mother

Trace and Practice

Variations

お お お お お

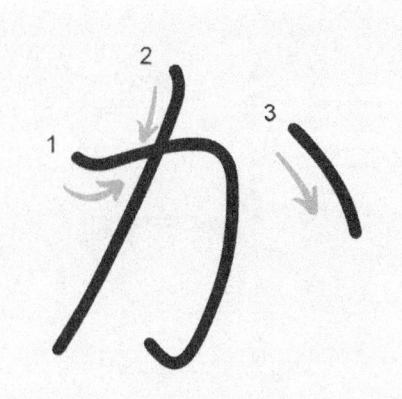

Stroke Order
Stroke Progression
Example Word

か

Ka
"Ca" as in "cart"
IPA: /ka/

かんごし

Kangoshi

Translation: Nurse

Trace and Practice
Variations

Ki

"Key" as in "key"

IPA: /ki/

Stroke Order

Stroke Progression

⸍ ⸺ き き

Example Word

きいろい

Kīroi

Translation: Yellow

Trace and Practice

Variations

き き き き き き

11

Stroke Order

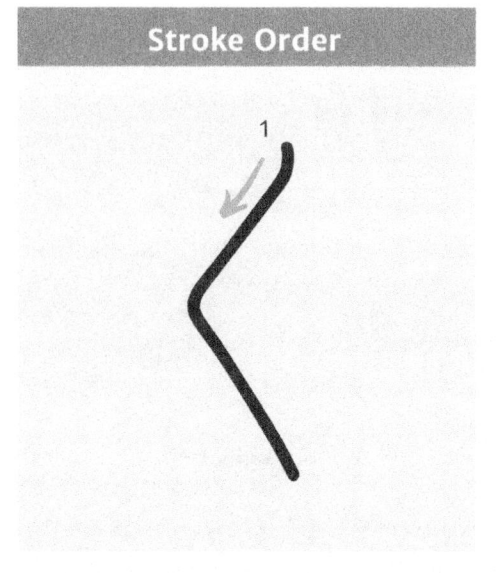

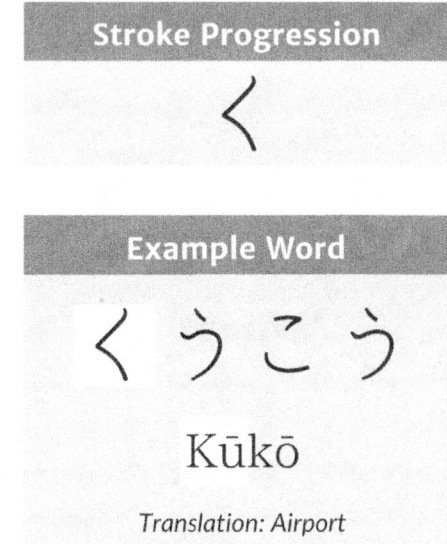

Stroke Progression

Example Word

くうこう

Kūkō

Translation: Airport

Ku

"Coo" as in "cool"

IPA: /kɯ/

Trace and Practice

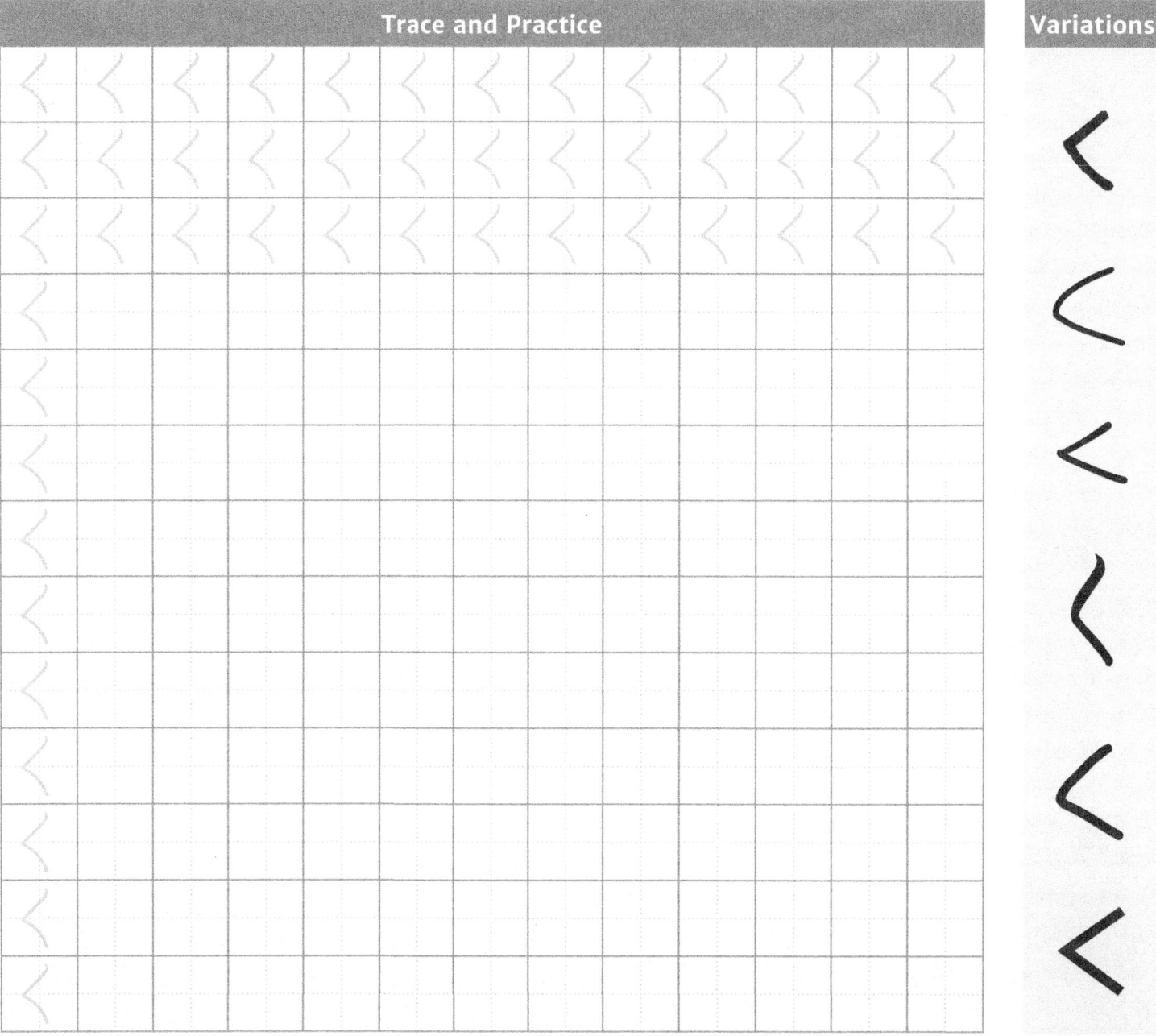

Variations

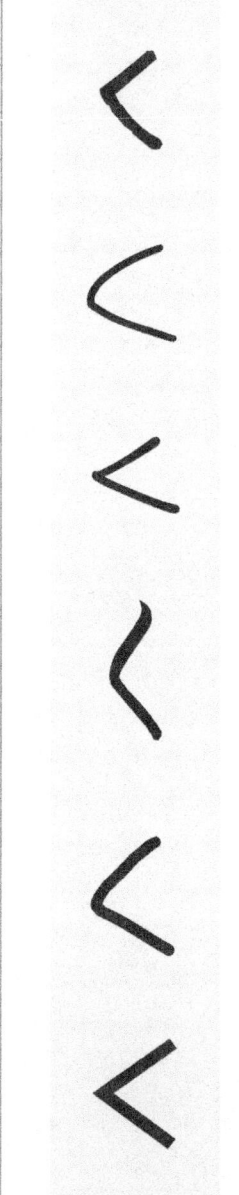

け
Ke

Similar to "Ke" as in "Kettle"
IPA: /ke/

Stroke Order

Stroke Progression

し に け

Example Word

けつだん

Ketsudan

Translation: Decision

Trace and Practice

Variations

けけけけけけ

こ

Ko

Similar to "ko" as in "Korea"

IPA: /ko/

Stroke Order

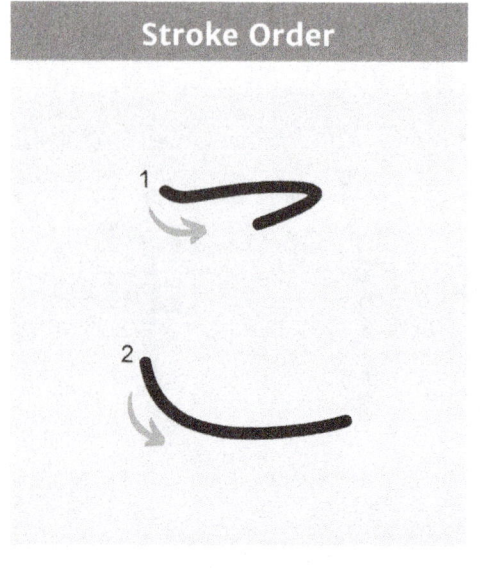

Stroke Progression

Example Word

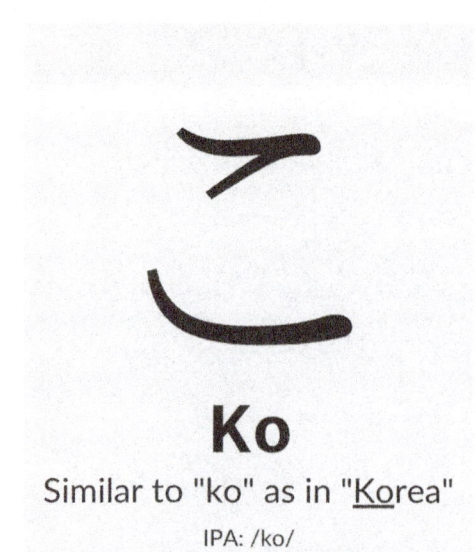

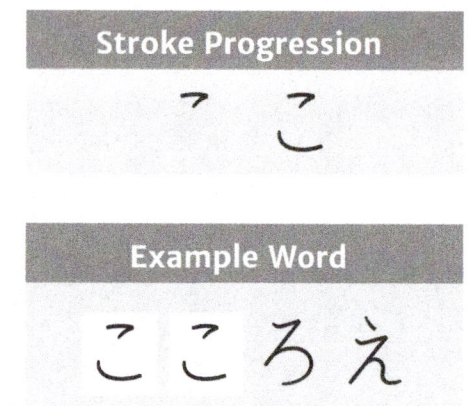

こころえ

Kokoroe

Translation: Information / Knowledge

Trace and Practice

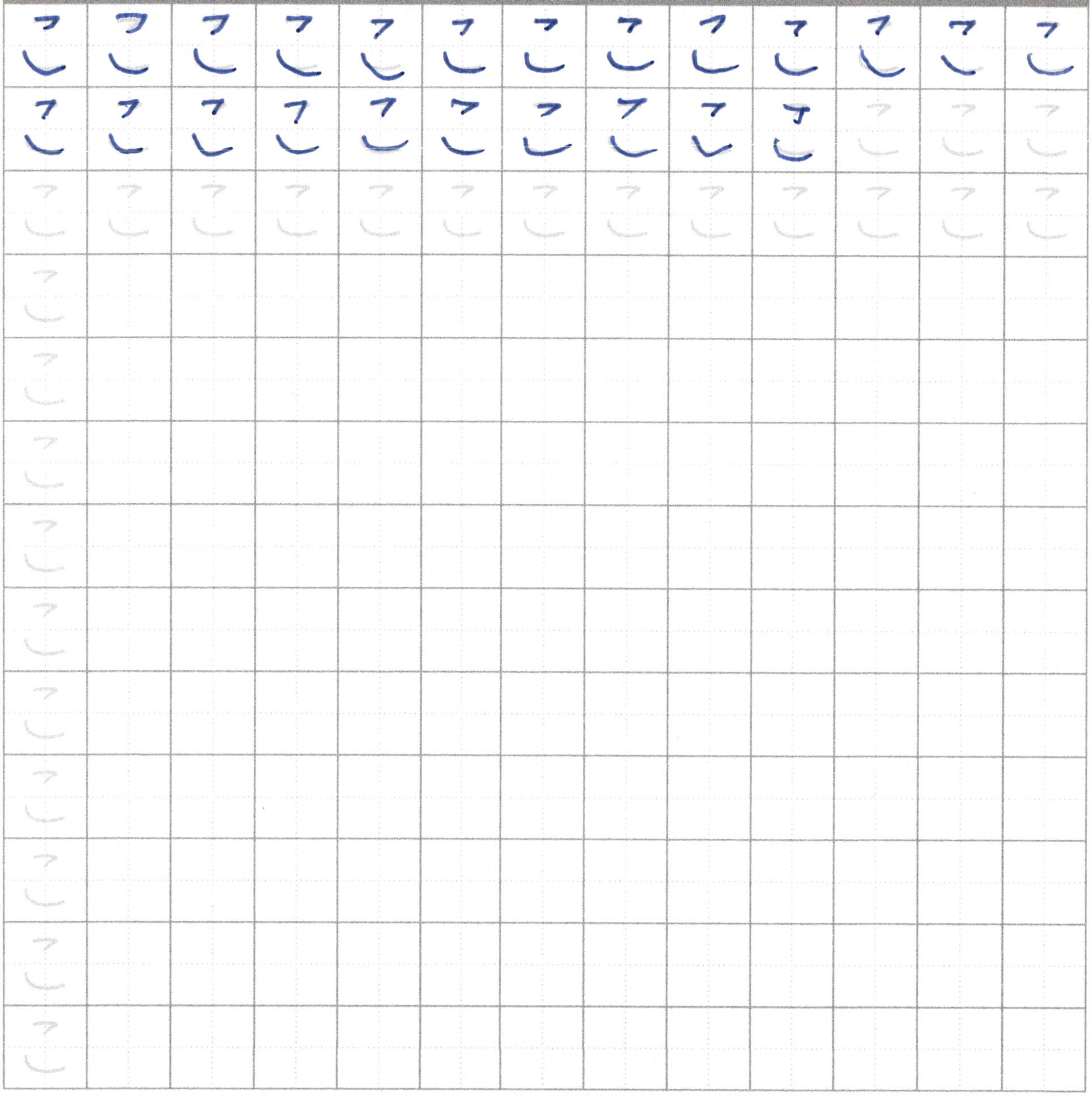

Variations

Sa

さ

Sa
"Sa" as in "salsa"
IPA: /sa/

Stroke Order

Stroke Progression

一 さ さ

Example Word

さんがつ

Sangatsu

Translation: March

Trace and Practice

Variations

さ さ さ さ さ

15

Stroke Order

Stroke Progression

Example Word

し

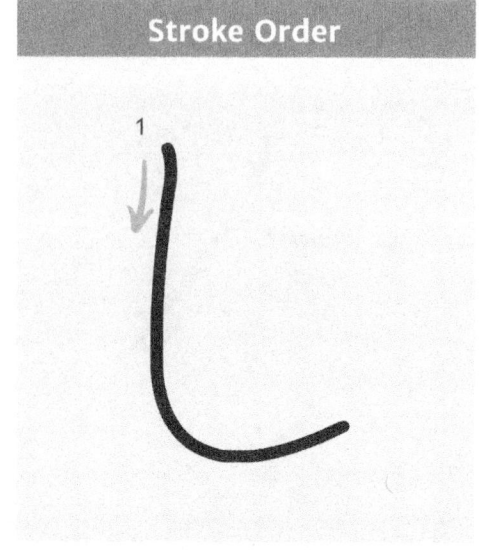

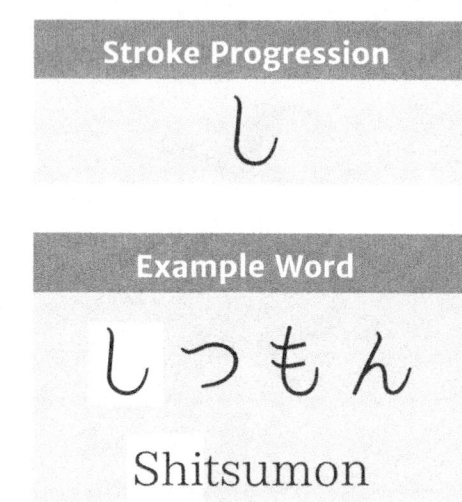

Shi

"She" as in "she"

IPA: /çi/

しつもん

Shitsumon

Translation: March

Trace and Practice

Variations

16

す
Su

"Su" as in "suchi"

IPA: /sɯ/

Stroke Order

Stroke Progression
一 す

Example Word
すいよう

Suiyō

Translation: Wednesday

Trace and Practice

Variations
す あ す す す す

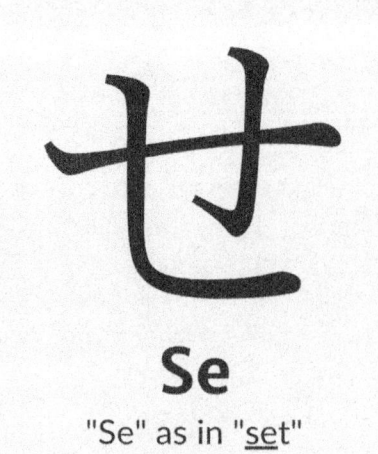

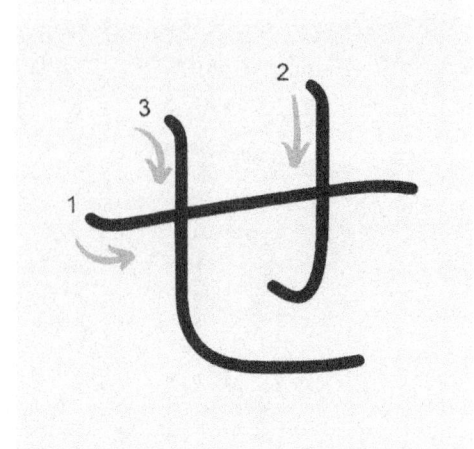

Stroke Order
Stroke Progression
Example Word

せ

Se
"Se" as in "set"
IPA: /se/

せんせい

Sensei

Translation: Teacher

Trace and Practice
Variations

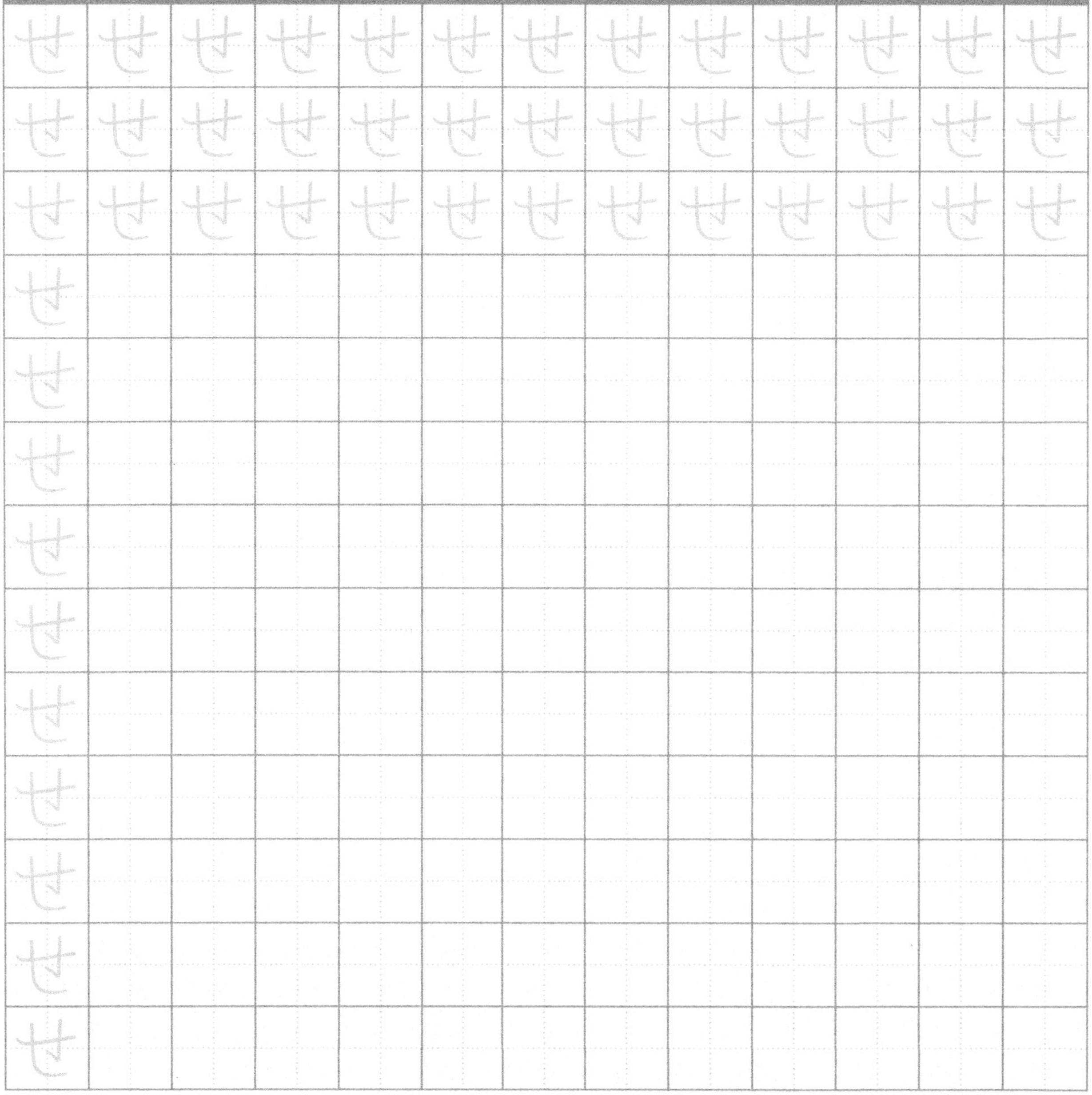

そ

So
"So" as in "so"
IPA: /so/

Stroke Order

Stroke Progression
そ

Example Word
それとも
Soretomo
Translation: Or / Or else

Trace and Practice

Variations

19

た

Ta
"Ta" as in "tall"
IPA: /ta/

Stroke Order

Stroke Progression
一 ナ た た

Example Word
ただなか
Tadanaka
Translation: Middle

Trace and Practice

Variations
た た た た

ち
Chi

"Chea" as in "cheat"

IPA: /tɕi/

Stroke Order

Stroke Progression

Example Word

ちかづく

Chikadzuku

Translation: Approach / Get close to

Trace and Practice

Variations

Tsu

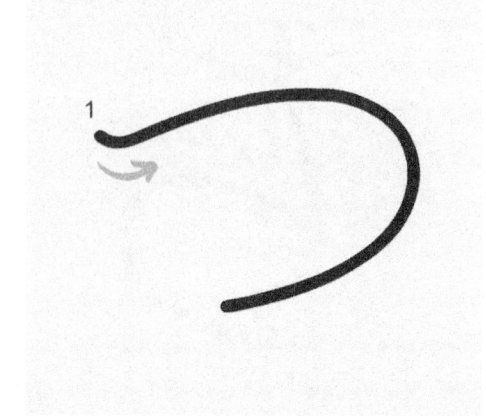

"Tsu" as in "tsunami"

IPA: /tsɯ/

Stroke Order

1

Stroke Progression

つ

Example Word

つめたい

Tsumetai

Translation: Cold / Unfriendly

Trace and Practice

Variations

22

Stroke Order

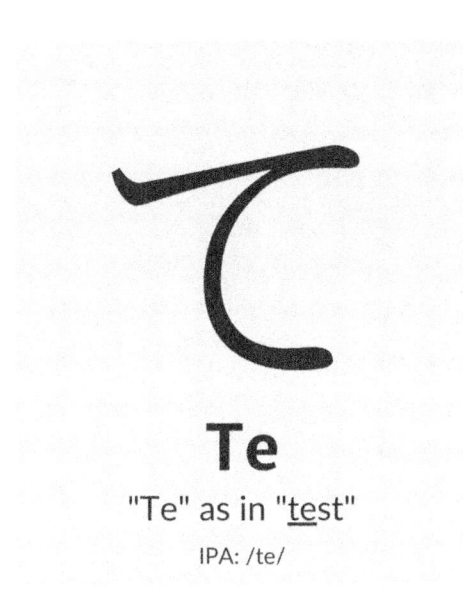

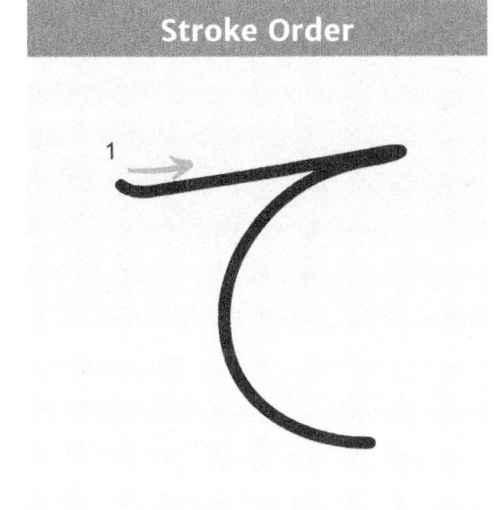

Stroke Progression
て

Example Word
てちょう

Techō

Translation: Notebook

Te

"Te" as in "test"

IPA: /te/

Trace and Practice

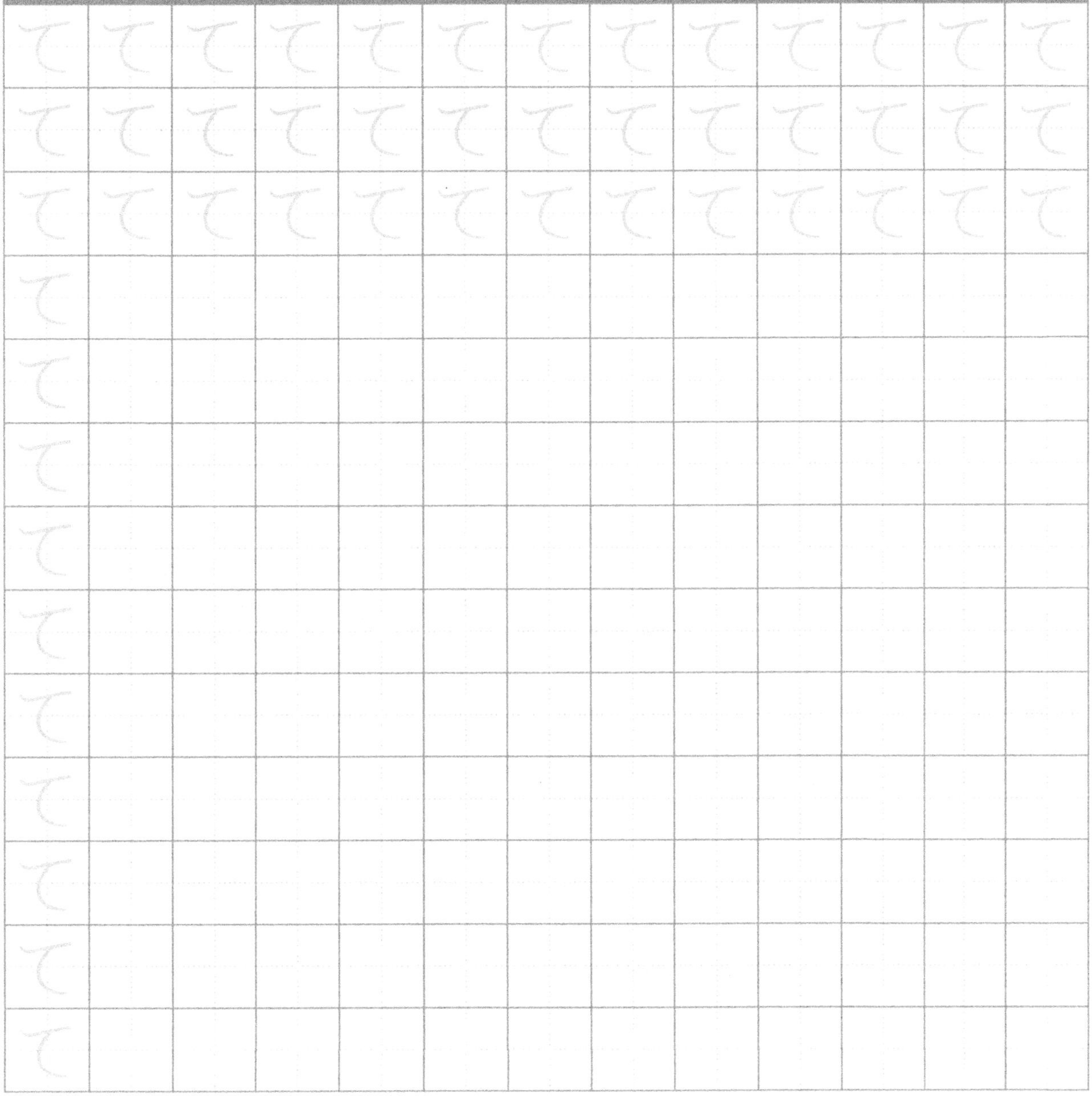

Variations

てててててて

と

To
"To" as in "toad"
IPA: /to/

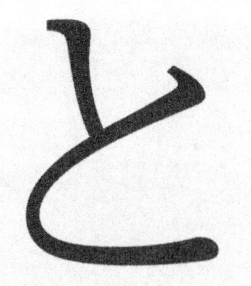

Stroke Order

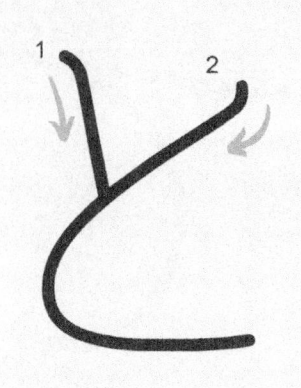

Stroke Progression
ー と

Example Word
ときどき
Tokidoki

Translation: Sometimes / At times

Trace and Practice

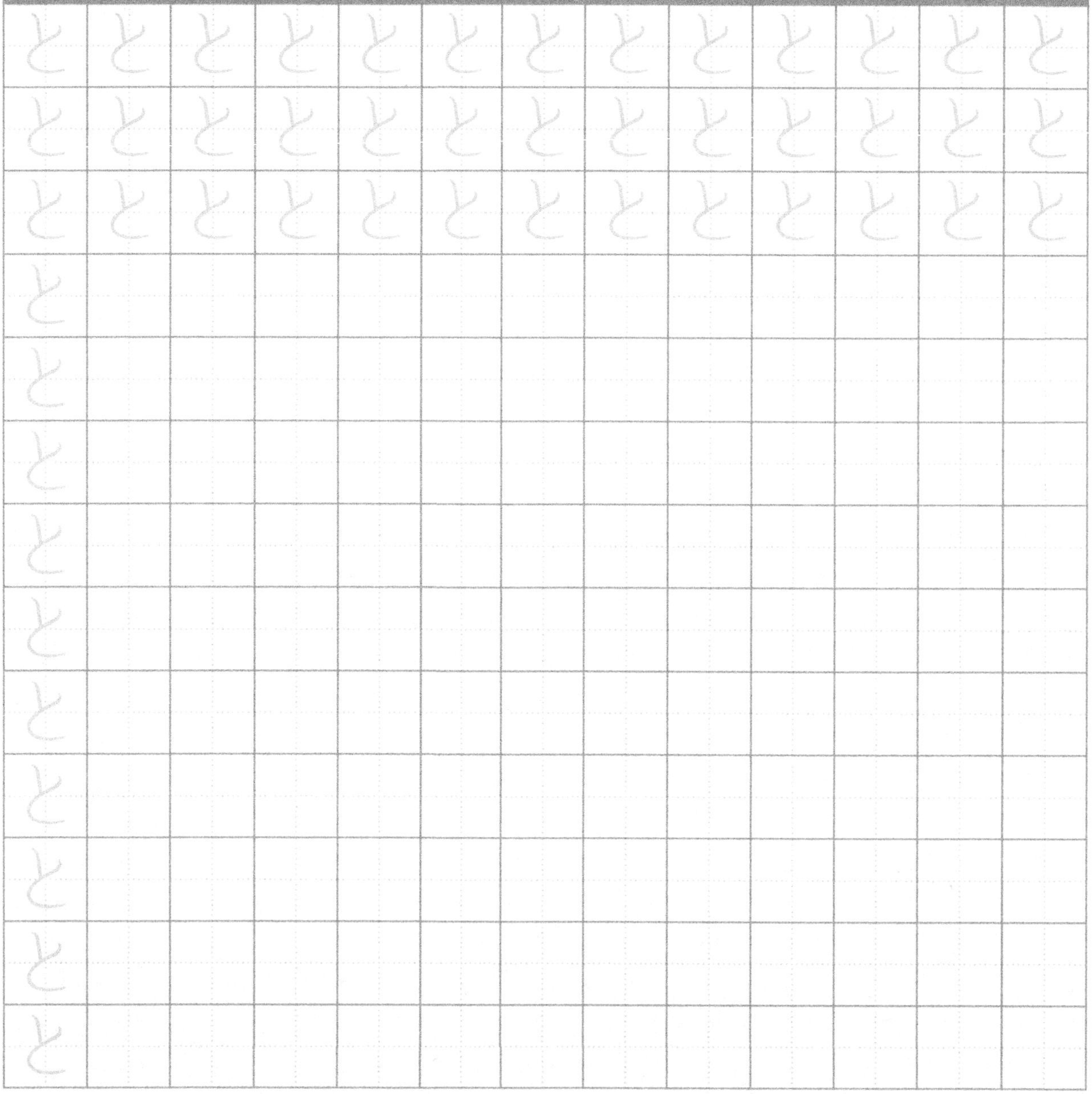

Variations
と と と と と と

Na

"Na" as in "nacho"

IPA: /na/

Stroke Order

Stroke Progression
一 ナ ナ な

Example Word
ならびに

Narabini

Translation: And / Together with

Trace and Practice

Variations
な な な な

Ni
"Knee" as in "Knee"
IPA: /ɲi/

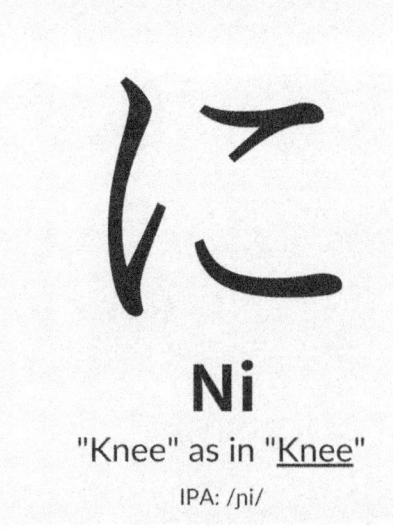

Stroke Order
に

Stroke Progression
い に に

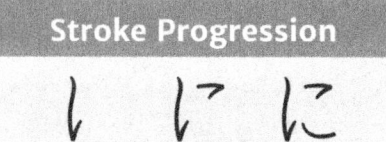

Example Word
にわとり
Niwatori

Translation: Domestic chicken

Trace and Practice

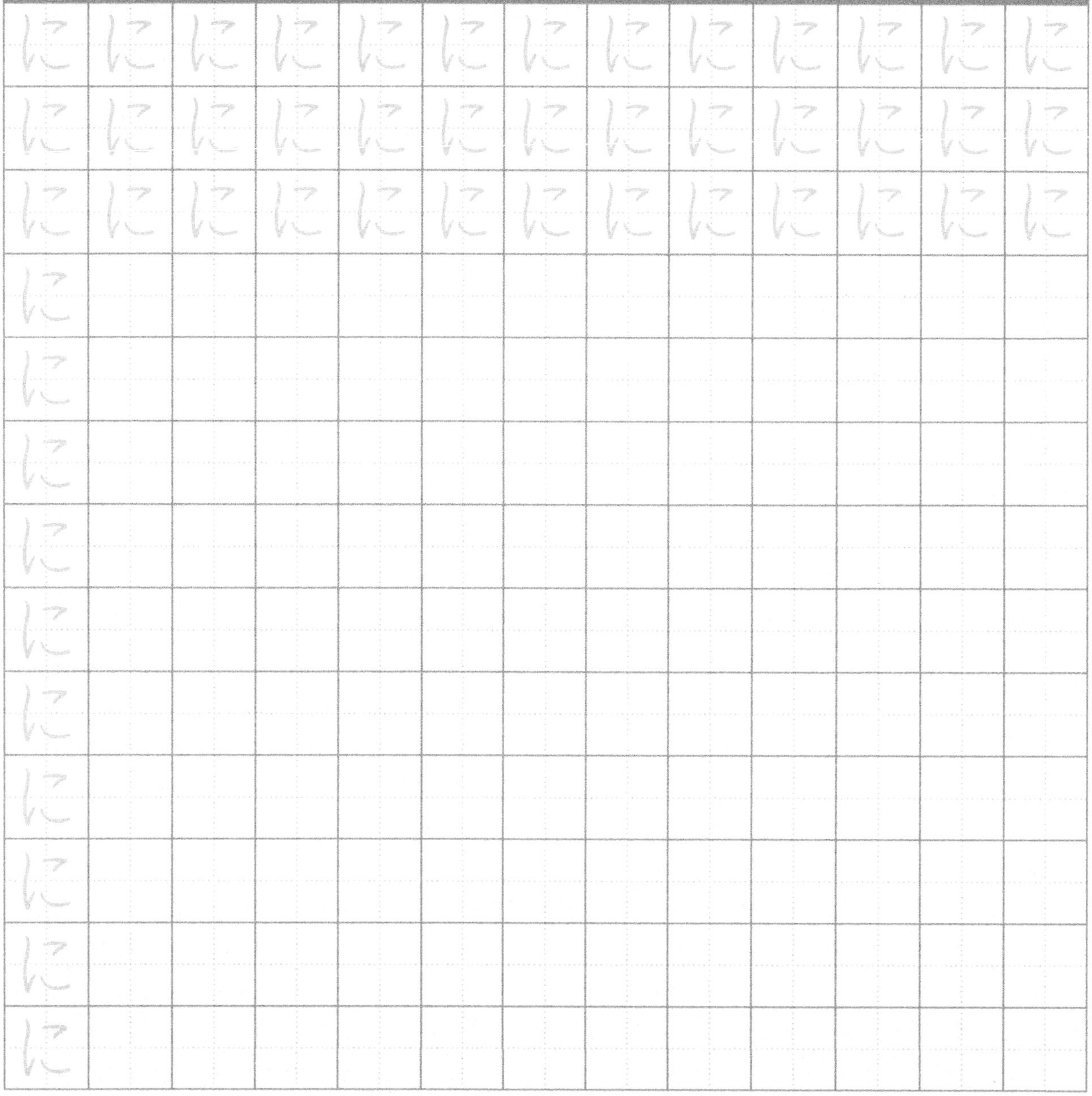

Variations
に に に に

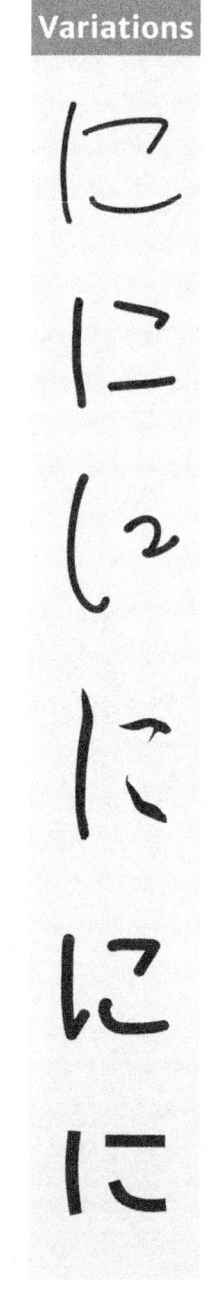

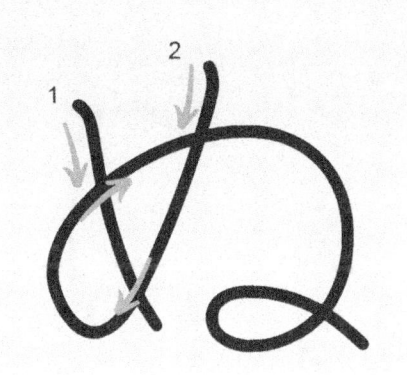

Stroke Order
Stroke Progression

ぬ

Nu
"Knew" as in "knew"
IPA: /nɯ/

Example Word

ぬくもり

Nukumori

Translation: Warmth

Trace and Practice

Variations

ね

Ne
"Ne" as in "Net"
IPA: /ne/

Stroke Order

Stroke Progression
｜ね

Example Word
ねぎらう
Negirau
Translation: Thank / Reward

Trace and Practice

Variations
ね ね ね ね ね ね

28

の

No

"No" as in "No"

IPA: /no/

Stroke Order

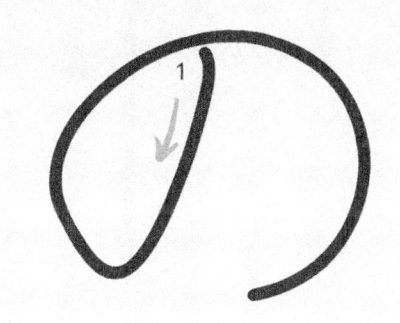

Stroke Progression

の

Example Word

のがれる

Nogareru

Translation: Escape

Trace and Practice

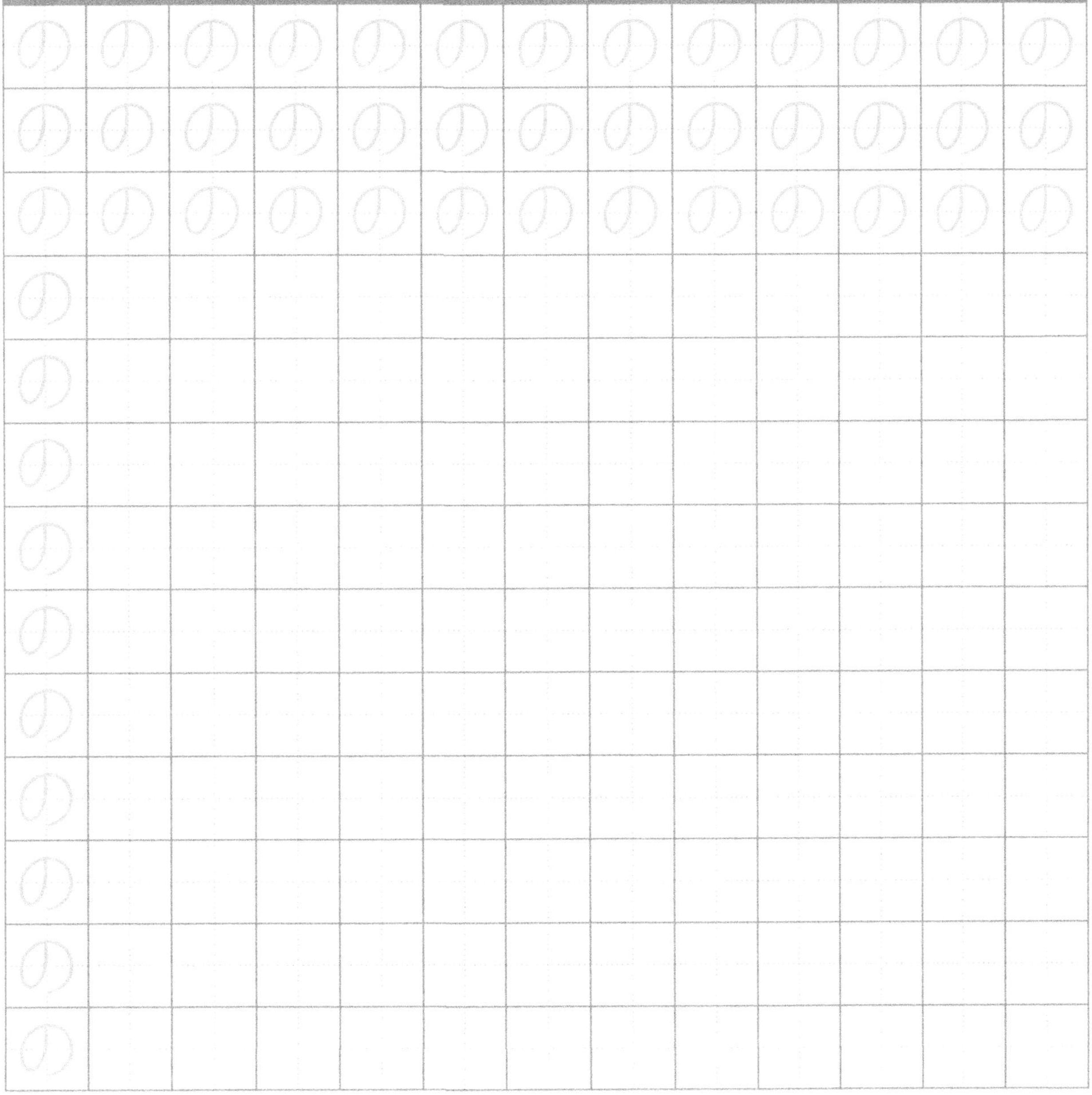

Variations

のののののの

Ha

"Ha" as in "haul"

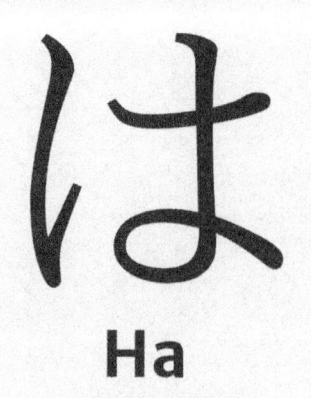

IPA: /ha/, /ɰa/ as particle

Stroke Order

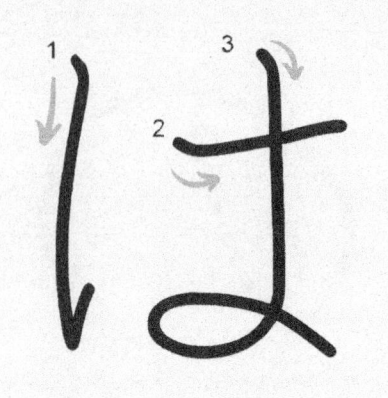

Stroke Progression

に は

Example Word

はいいろ

Haīro

Translation: Grey

Trace and Practice

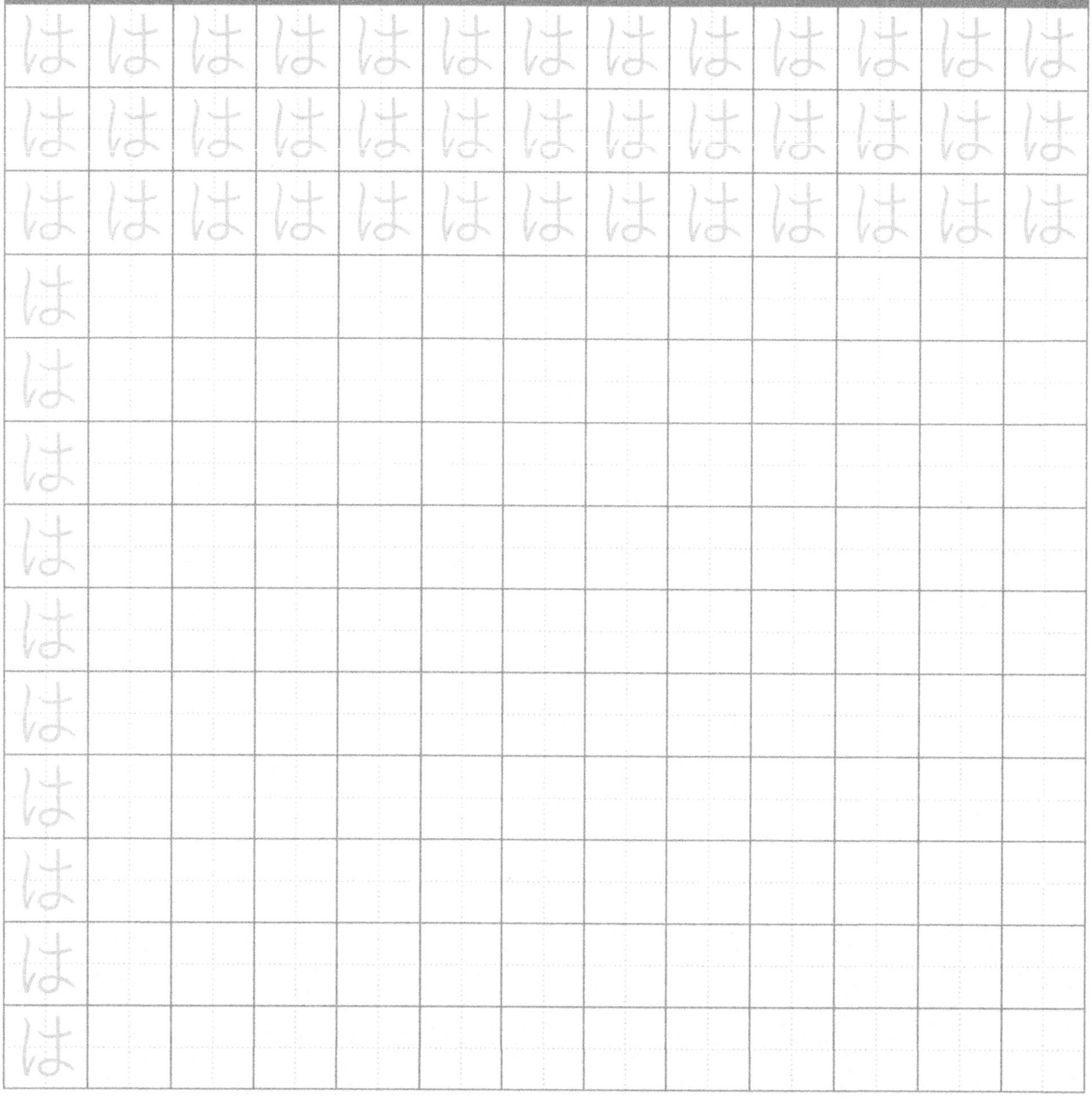

Variations

は は は は は

30

Stroke Order

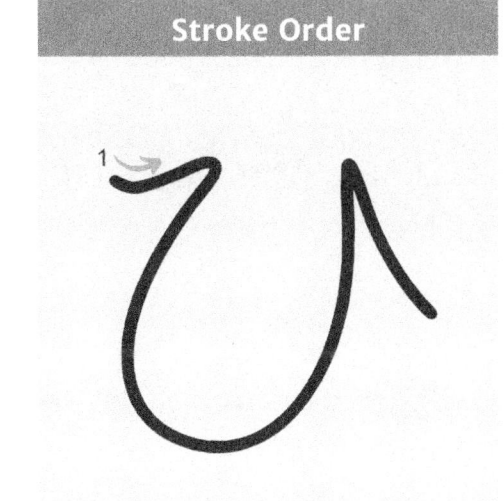

Stroke Progression

ひ

Example Word

ひこうき

Hikōki

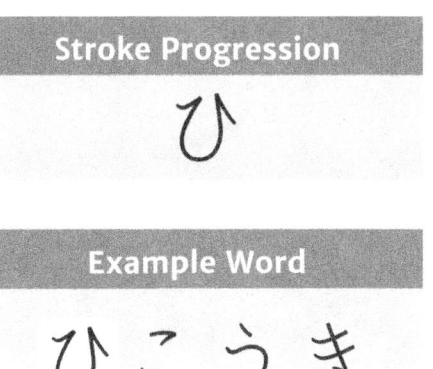

Translation: Airplane

Hi

"He" as in "he"

IPA: /çi/

Trace and Practice

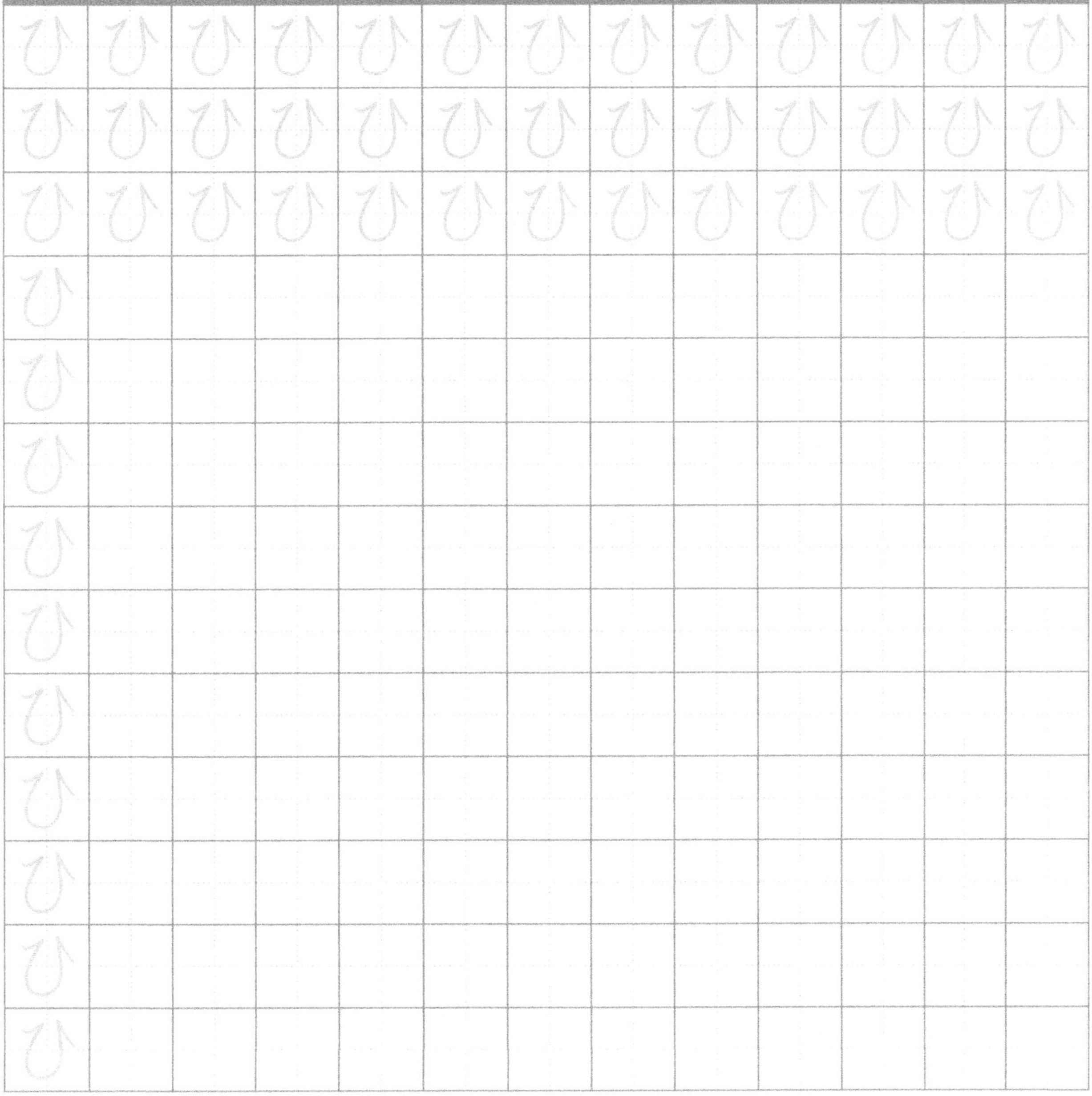

Variations

ひ ひ ひ ひ ひ ひ

31

ふ

Fu

"Foo" as in "Fool"

IPA: /ɸɯ/

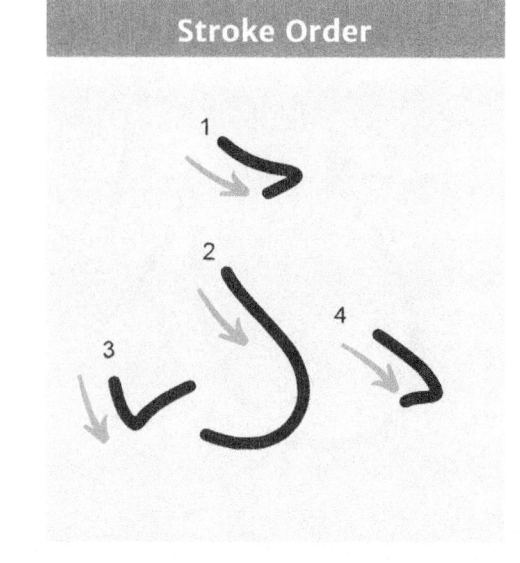

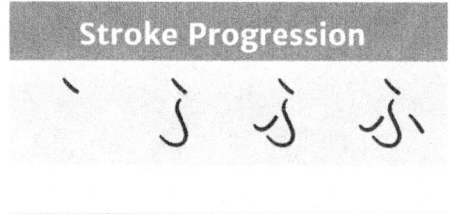

Stroke Order

Stroke Progression

丶 う ふ ふ

Example Word

ふかのう

Fukanō

Translation: Impossible

Trace and Practice

Variations

Stroke Order

Stroke Progression

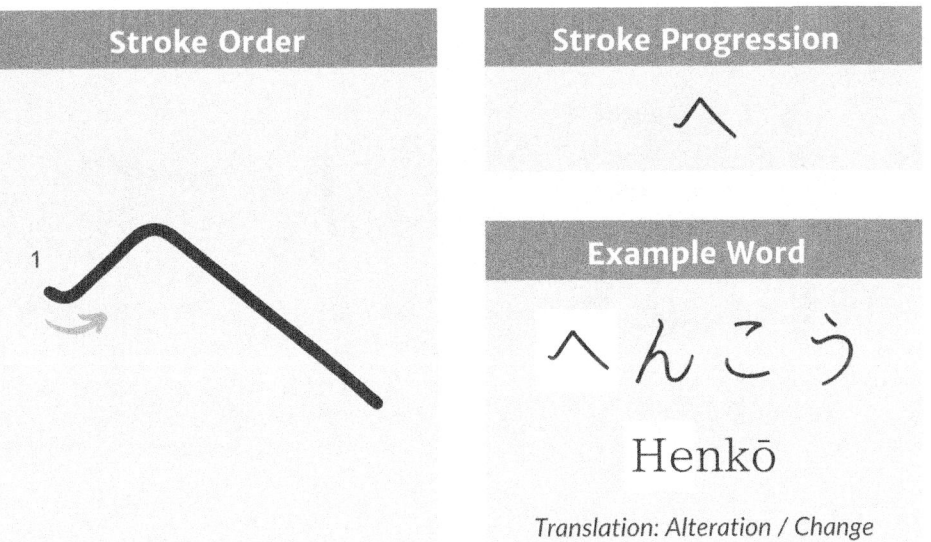

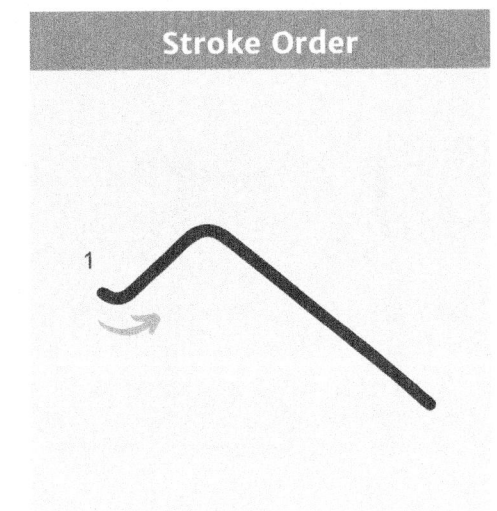

He
"He" as in "Head"
IPA: /he/, /e/ as a particle

Example Word

へんこう

Henkō

Translation: Alteration / Change

Trace and Practice

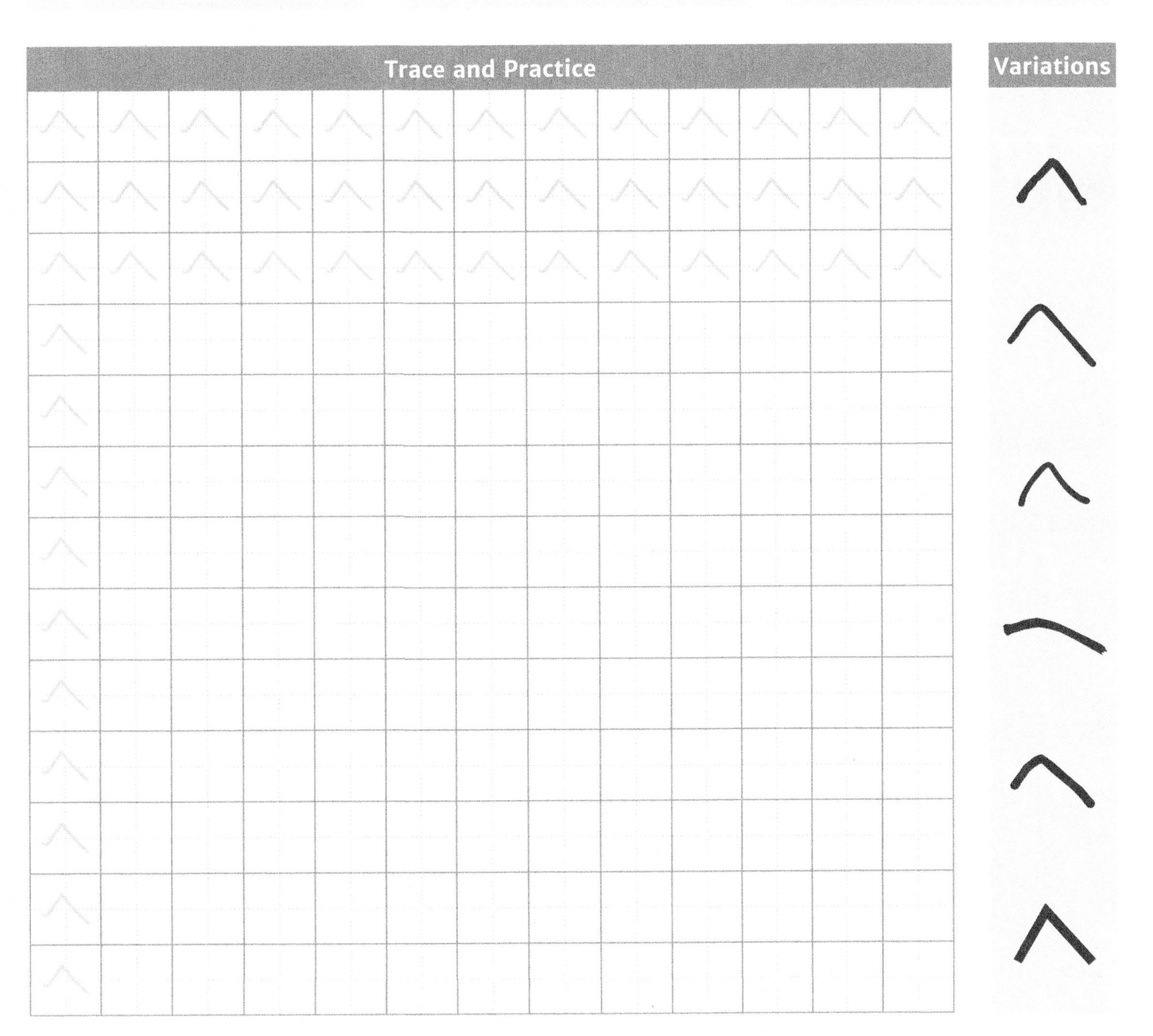

Variations

33

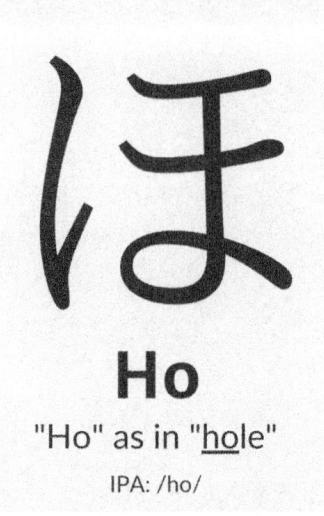

Stroke Order
Stroke Progression
ℓ   に   に   ほ

ほ
Ho
"Ho" as in "hole"
IPA: /ho/

Example Word
ほほえむ

Hohoemu

Translation: To smile

Trace and Practice

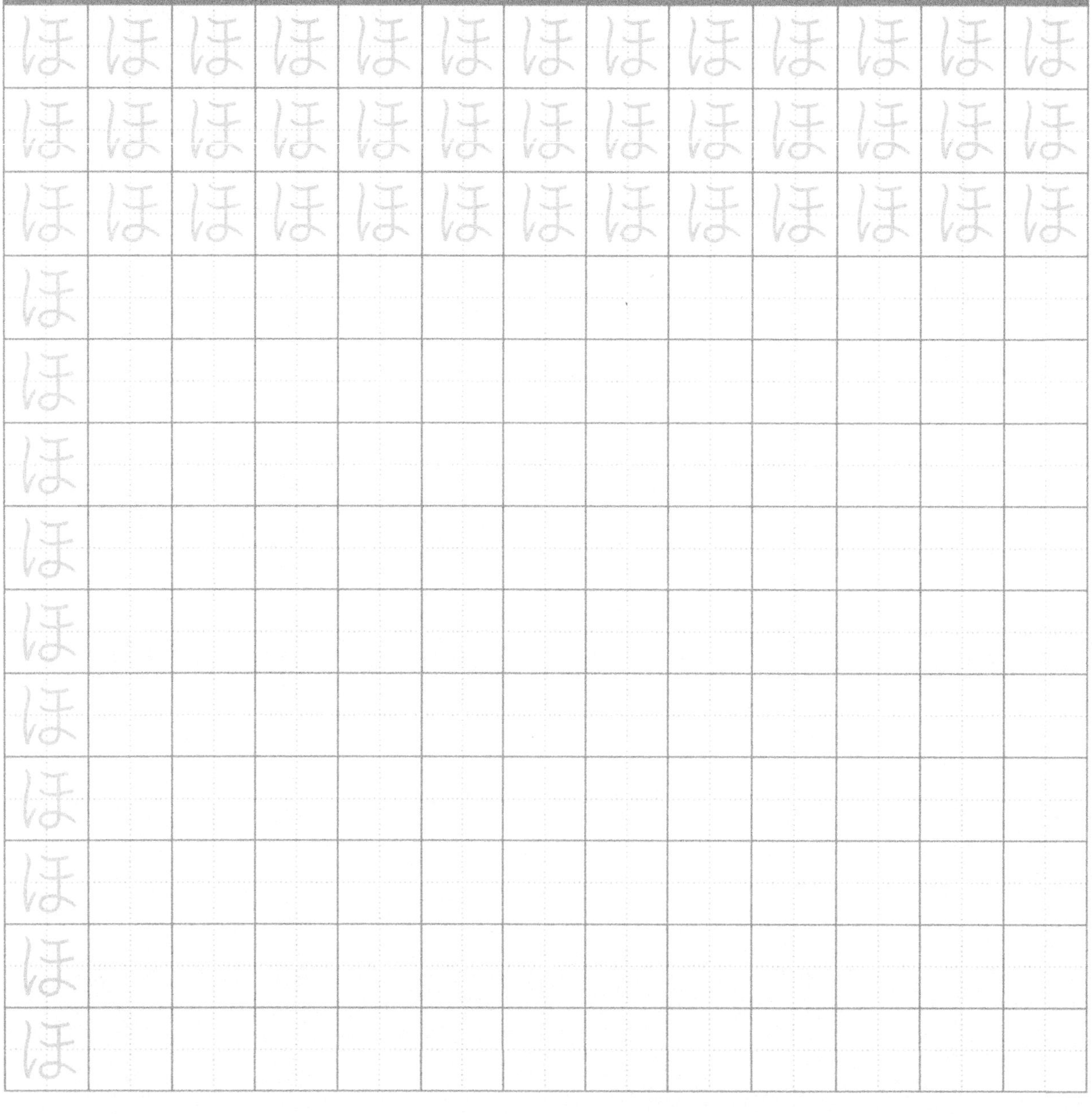

Variations
ほ
ほ
ほ
ほ
ほ
ほ

Ma

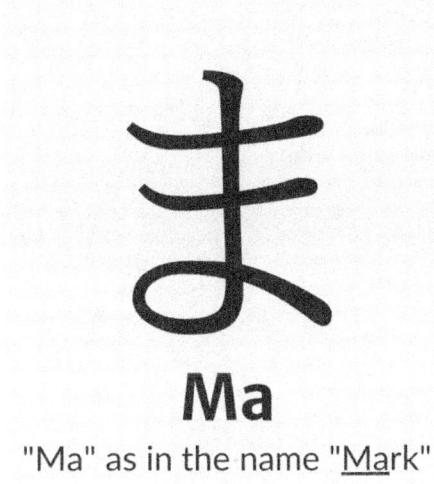

"Ma" as in the name "Mark"

IPA: /ma/

Stroke Order

Stroke Progression

一 二 ま

Example Word

まちがい

Machigai

Translation: Mistake

Trace and Practice

Variations

ま
ま
ま
ま
ま

Mi

み

"Mi" as in "milk"

IPA: /mi/

Stroke Order

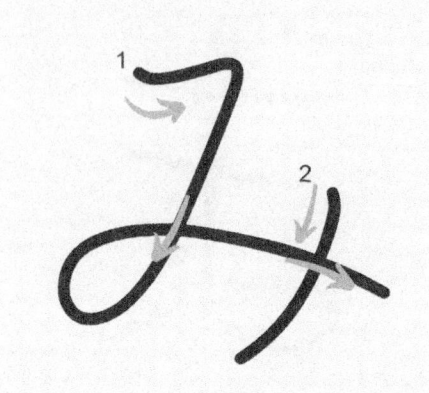

Stroke Progression

み み

Example Word

みずうみ

Mizuumi

Translation: Lake

Trace and Practice

Variations

み み み み み み

Stroke Order

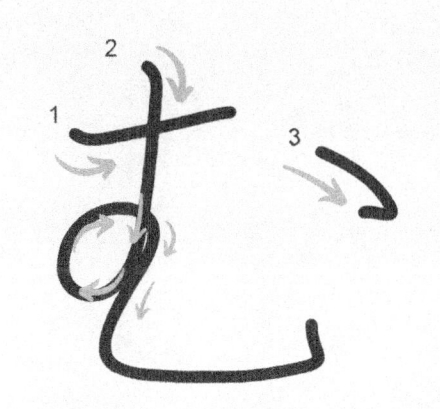

Stroke Progression

　 む む

Example Word

むなしい

Munashii

Translation: Empty / Futile

Mu

"Moo" as in "Moon"

IPA: /mɯ/

Trace and Practice

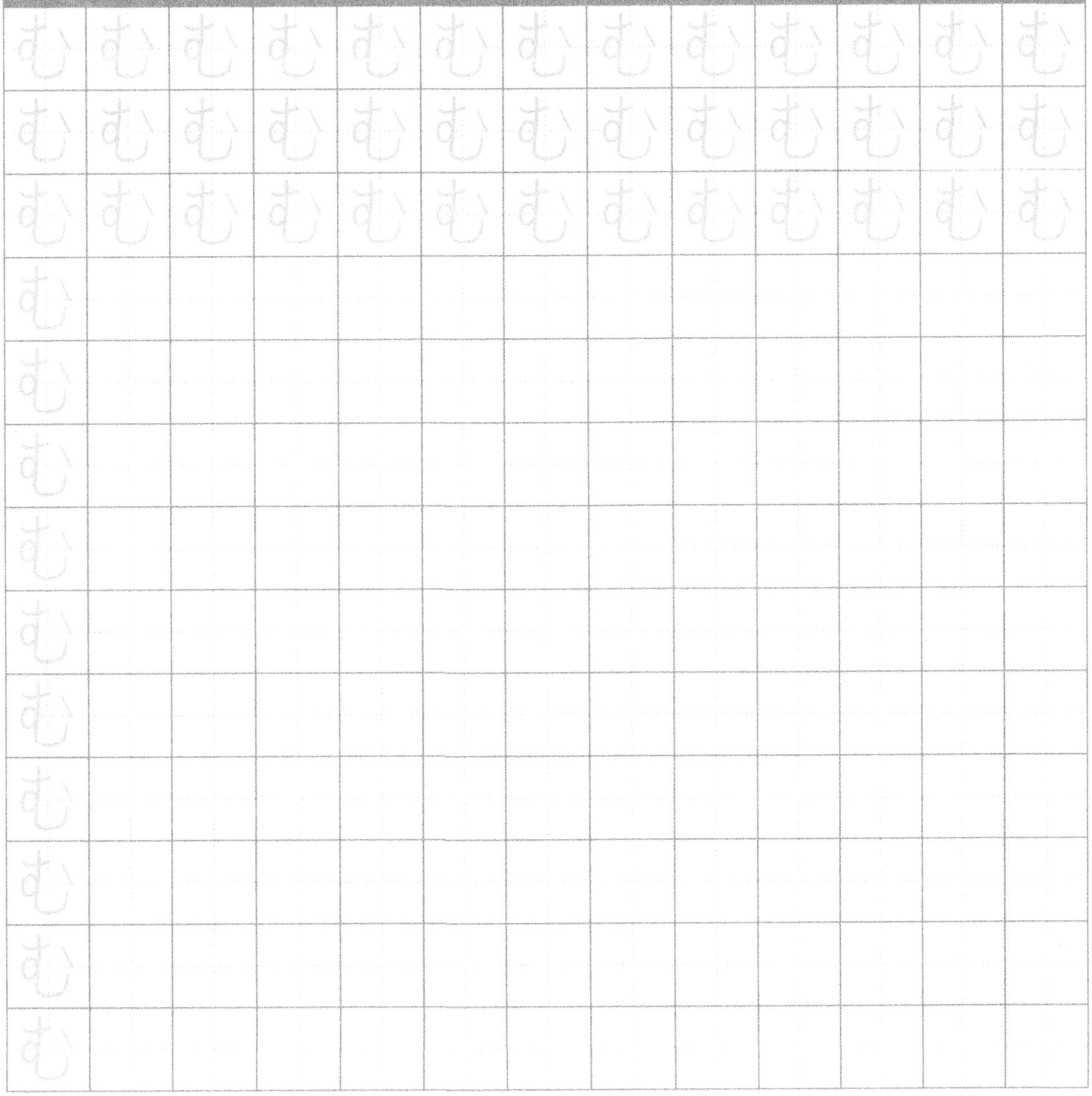

Variations

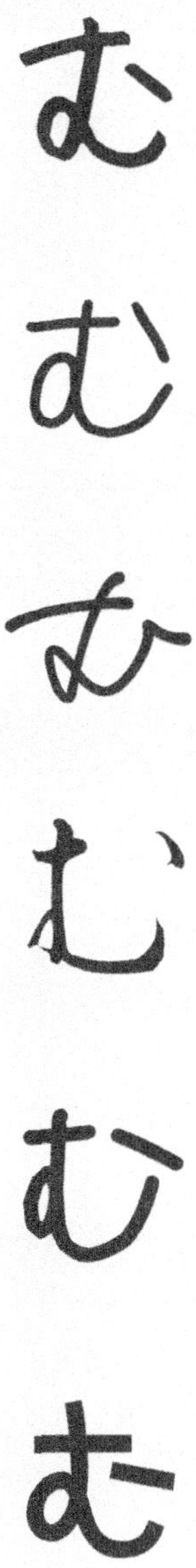

む む む む む む

37

Me

め

"Me" as in "Met"

IPA: /me/

Stroke Order

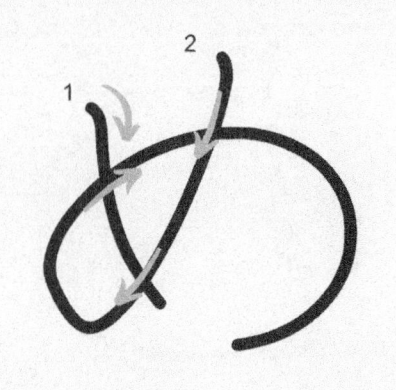

Stroke Progression
ノ め

Example Word
めいさく

Meisaku

Translation: Masterpiece

Trace and Practice

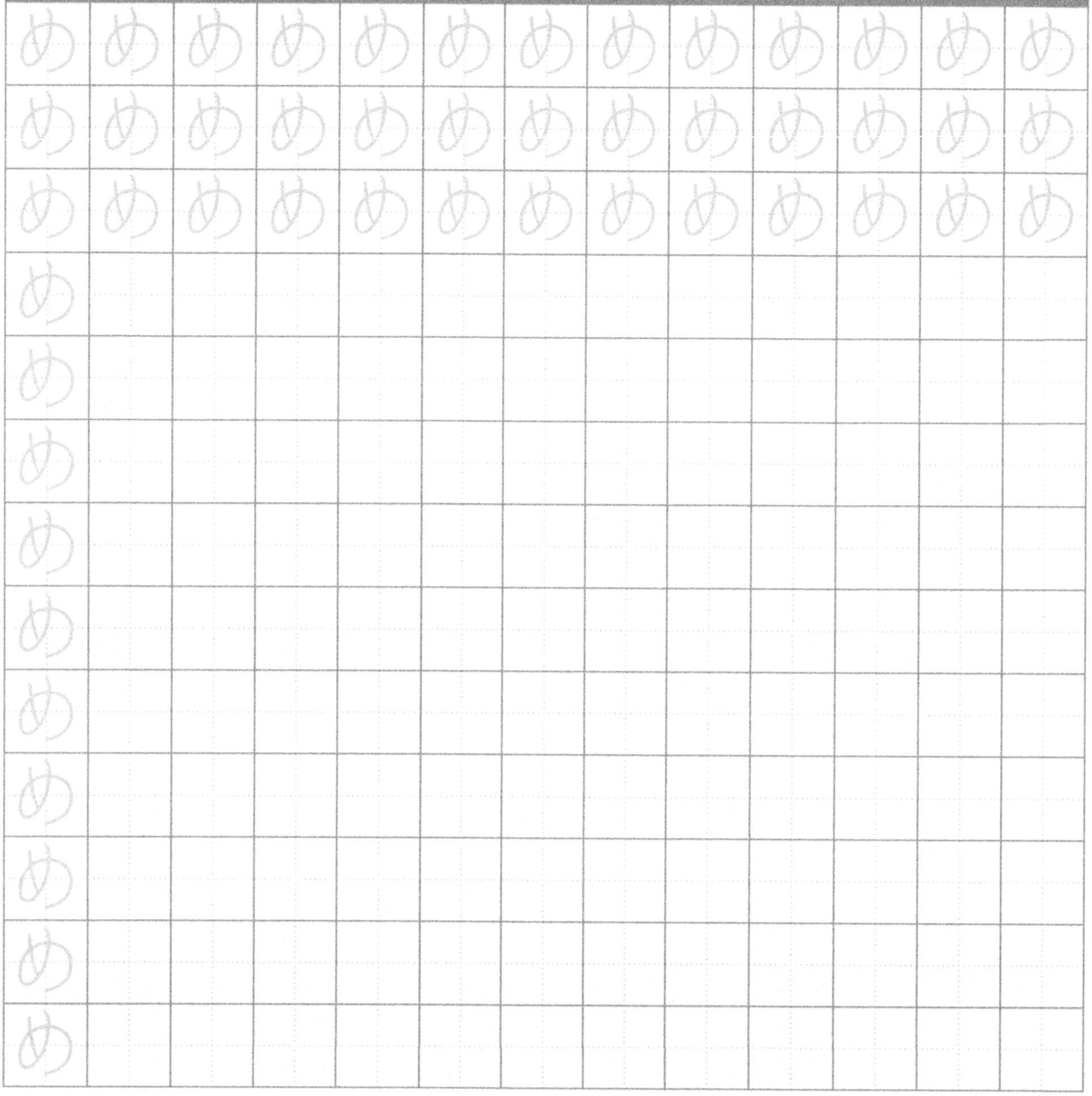

Variations

38

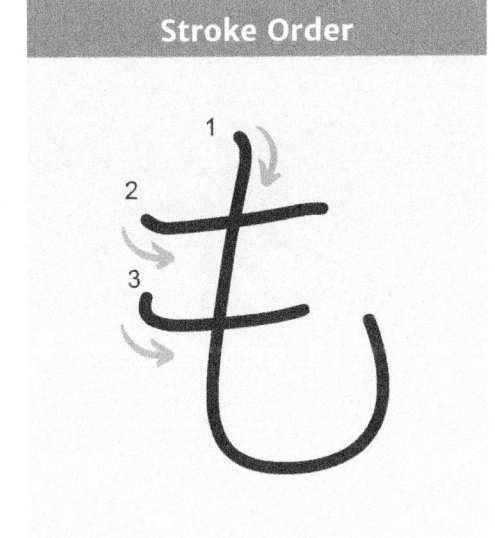

Stroke Order
Stroke Progression
し も も

Example Word
もんだい

Mondai

Translation: Problem / Question

も
Mo
Similar to "ko" as in "Korea"
IPA: /ko/

Trace and Practice

Variations
も も も と も も

Ya

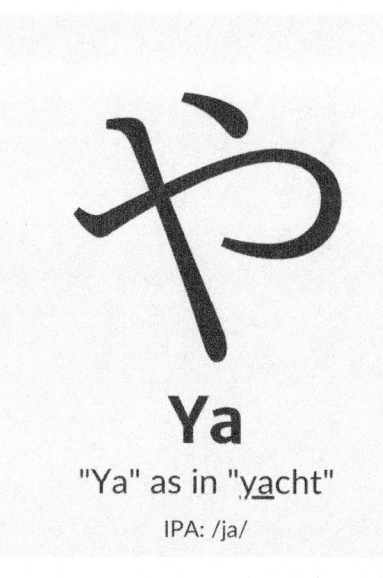

Ya — "Ya" as in "yacht"
IPA: /ja/

Stroke Order

Stroke Progression
っ う や

Example Word
やっぱり
Yappari
Translation: As expected / As well

Trace and Practice

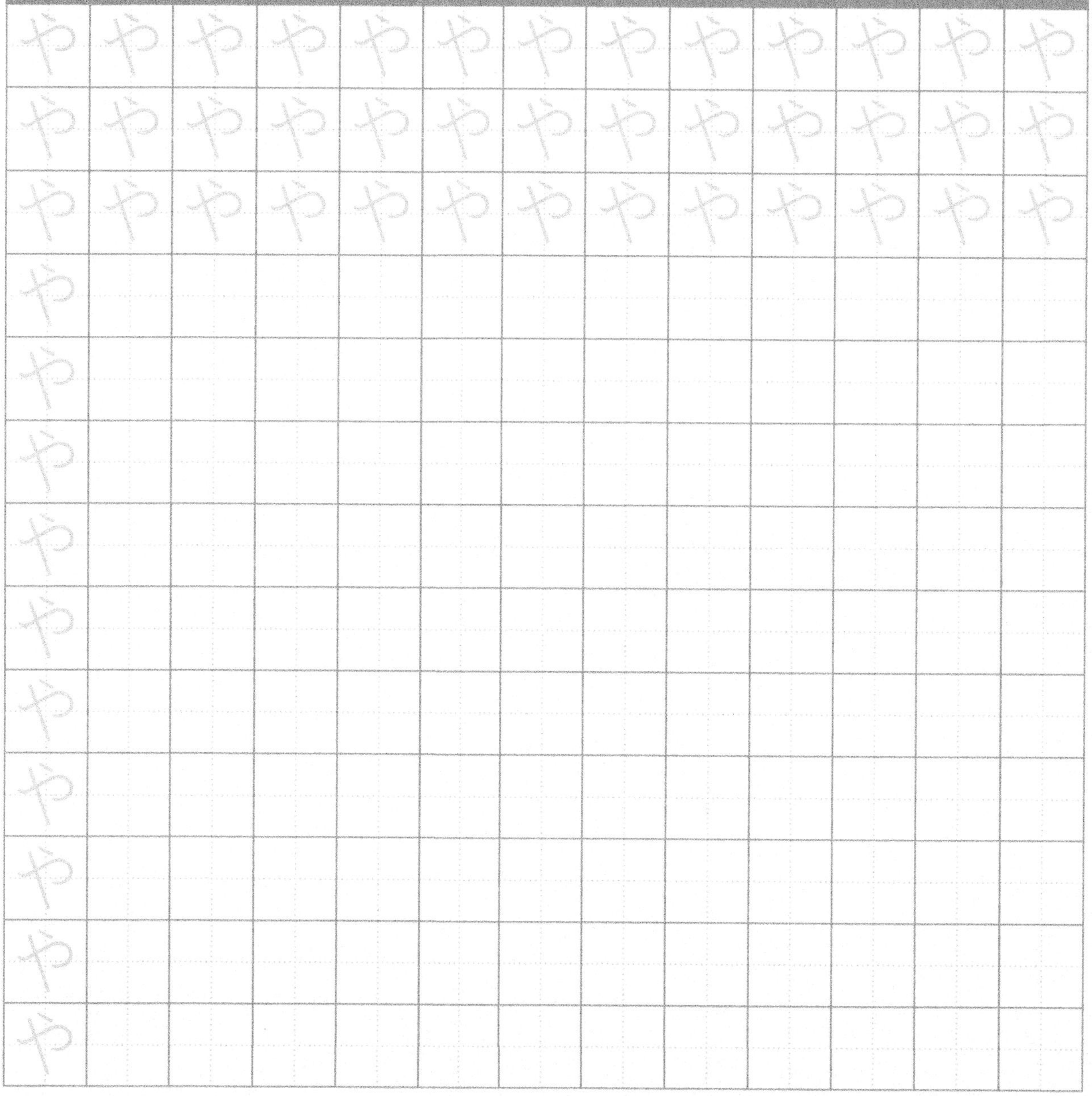

Variations
や や や や や や

Yu

ゆ

Yu

"You" as in "you"

IPA: /yɯ/

Stroke Order

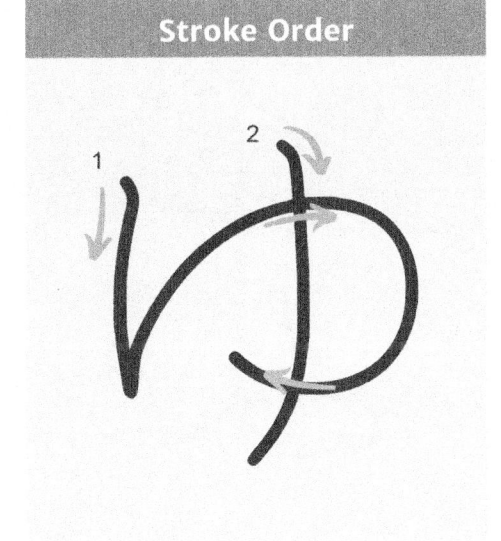

Stroke Progression

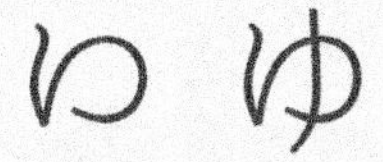

ゎ ゆ

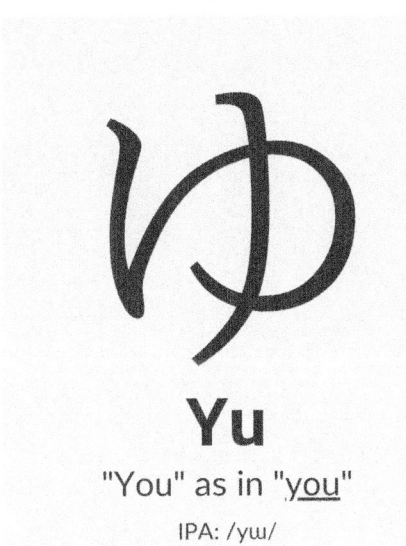

Example Word

ゆうはん

Yūhan

Translation: Dinner

Trace and Practice

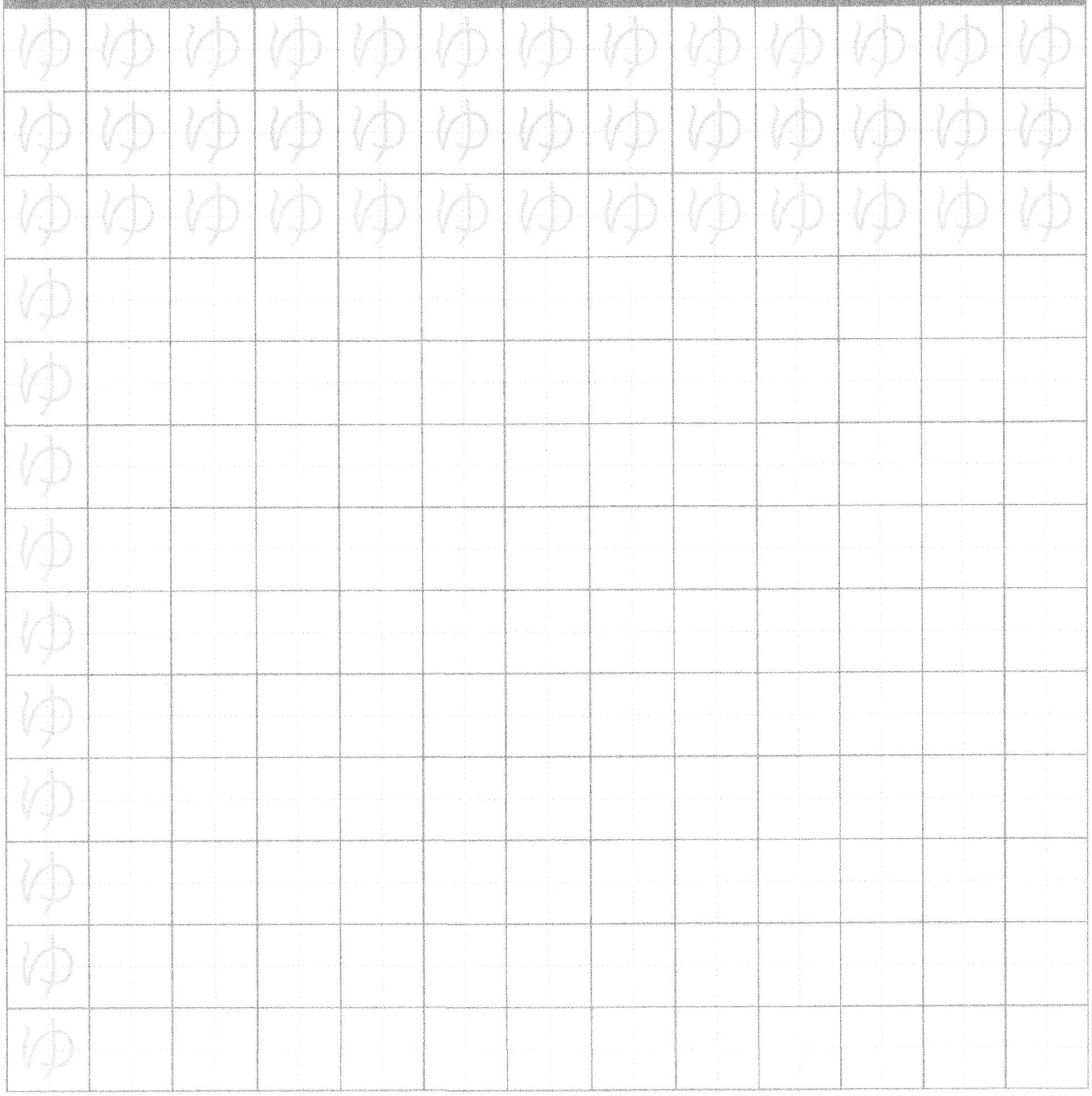

Variations

41

Yo
"Yo" as in "York"
IPA: /jo/

Stroke Order

Stroke Progression
一 よ

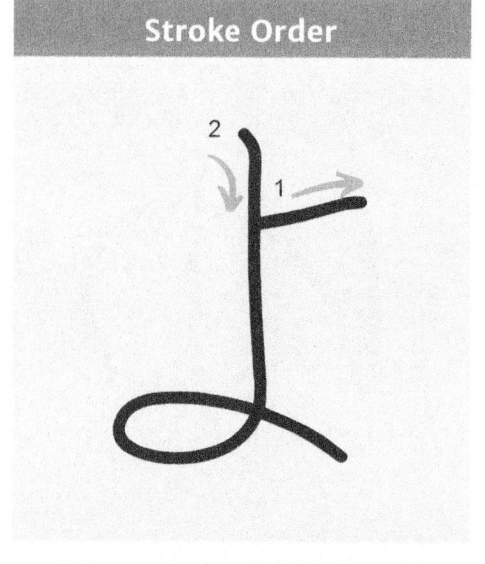

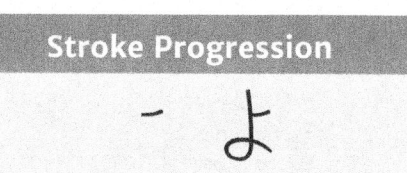

Example Word
よくしつ

Yokupoopsu

Translation: Bathroom

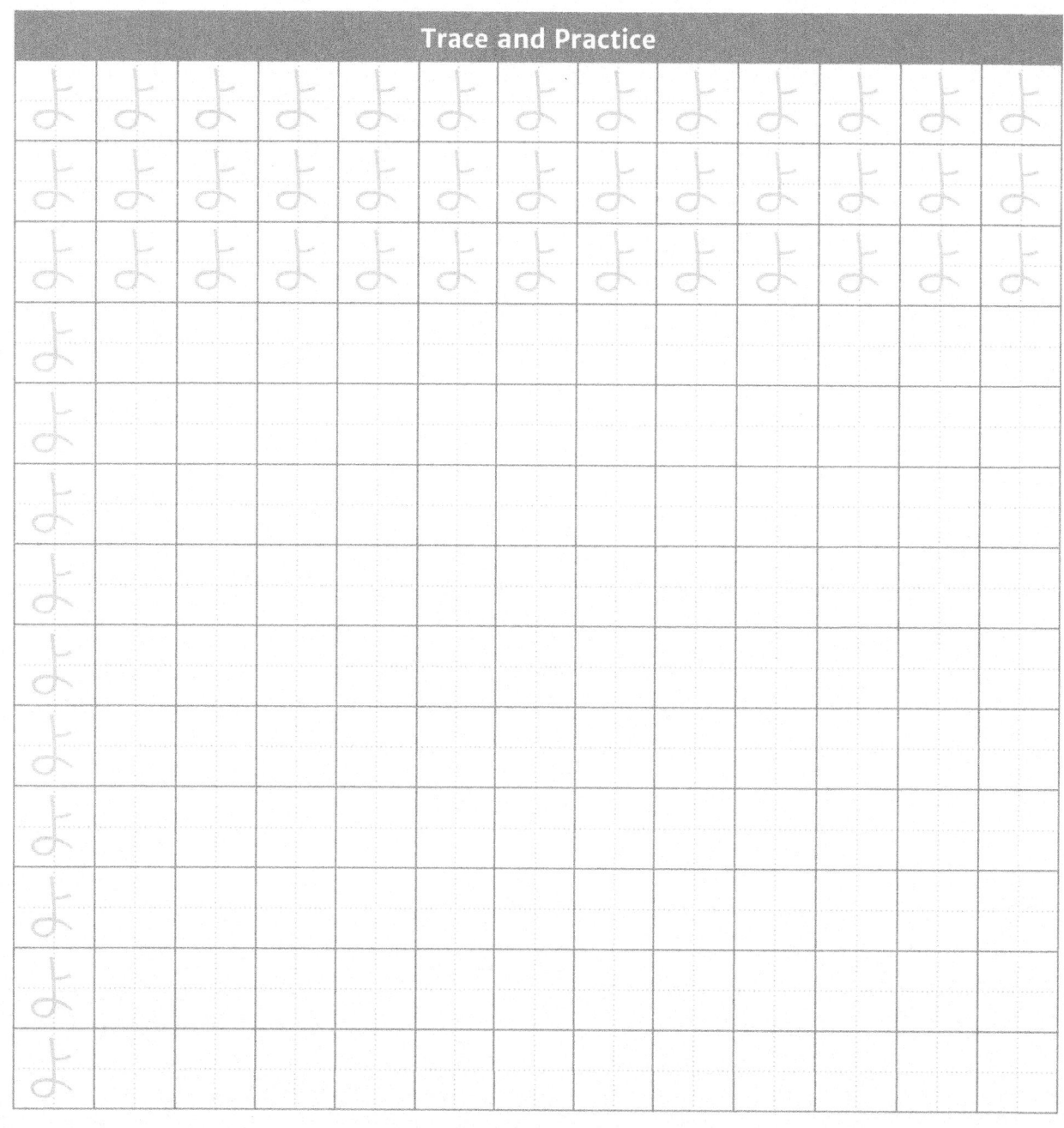

Trace and Practice

Variations

Stroke Order

Stroke Progression

Example Word

らくてん

Rakuten

Translation: Optimism

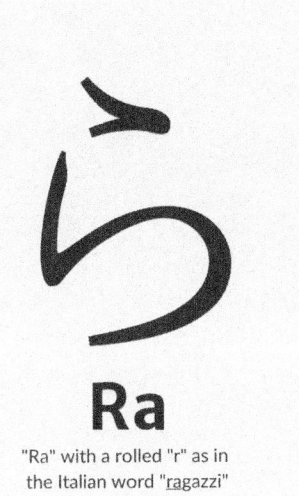

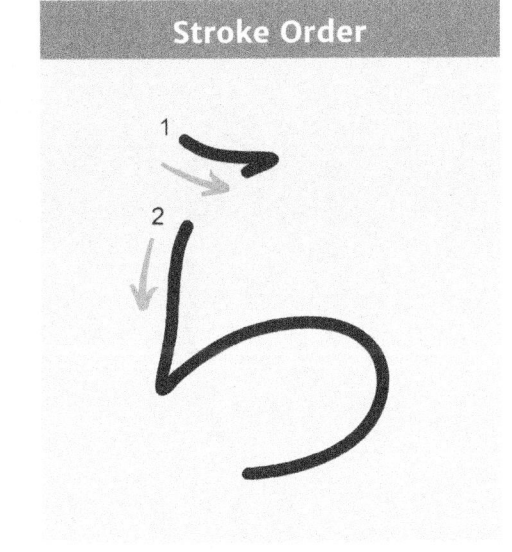

Ra

"Ra" with a rolled "r" as in the Italian word "ragazzi"

IPA: /ra/

Trace and Practice

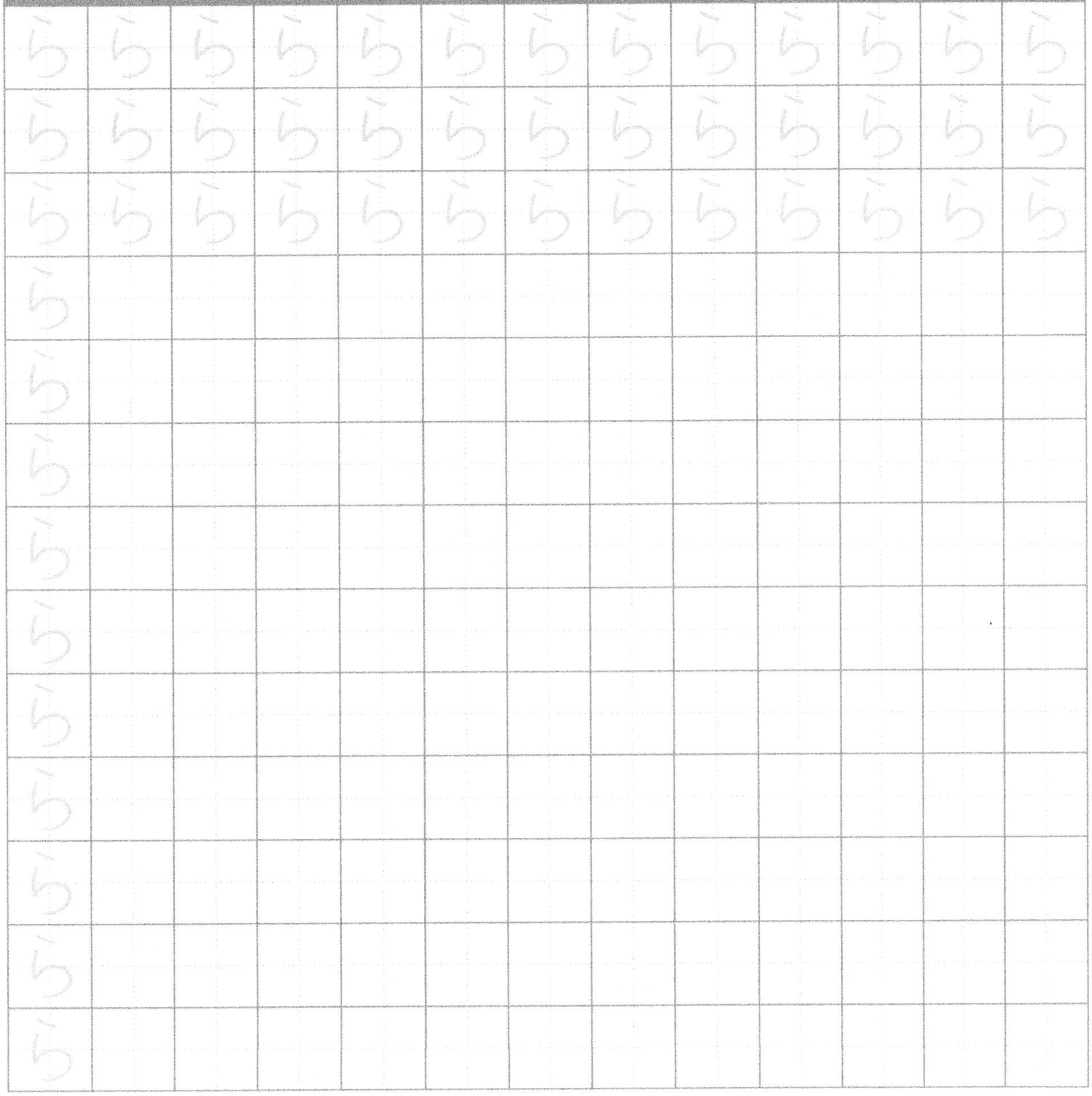

Variations

43

り

Chi

Rolled "r" as in the Italian word "ragazzi" pronounced together with an "i" as in "Italy"

IPA: /ri/

Stroke Order

Stroke Progression

Example Word

りんかい

Rinkai

Translation: Seaside

Trace and Practice

Variations

Ru

Rolled "r" as in the Italian word "ragazzi" pronounced together with an "Oo" as in "zoo"

IPA: /ɾɯ/

Stroke Order

Stroke Progression

る

Example Word

るすばん

Rusuban

Translation: Caretaker / Care-taking

Trace and Practice

Variations

45

Re

Rolled "r" as in the Italian word "ragazzi" pronounced together with an "e" as in "set"

IPA: /re/

Stroke Order

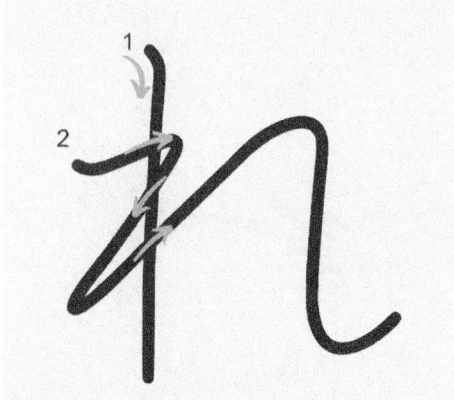

Stroke Progression

丨 れ

Example Word

れんあい

Ren'ai

Translation: Love / Compassion

Trace and Practice

Variations

Stroke Order

Stroke Progression

Example Word

ろくがつ

Rokugatsu

Translation: June

Ro

Rolled "r" as in the Italian word "ragazzi" pronounced together with an "o" as in "boat"

IPA: /ro/

Trace and Practice

Variations

47

Stroke Order

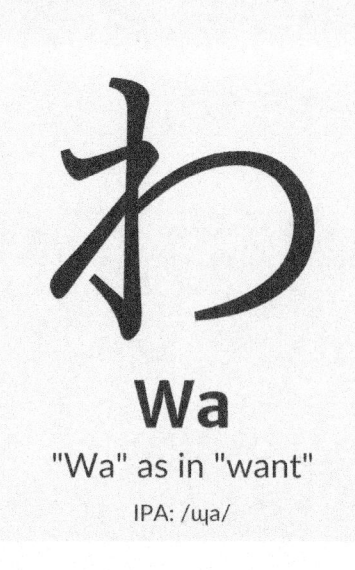

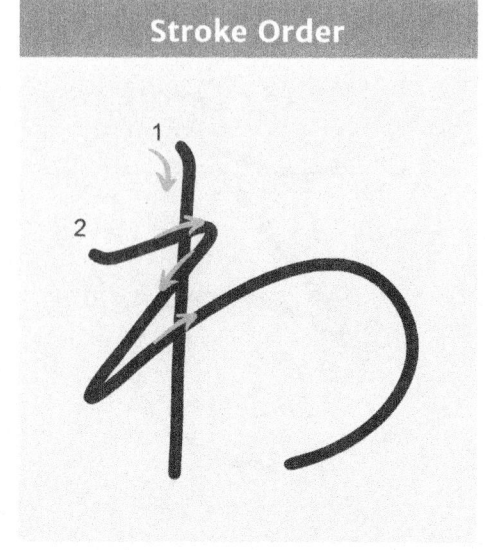

Stroke Progression

| わ

Example Word

わがまま

Wagamama

Translation: Selfish / Selfishness

わ
Wa
"Wa" as in "want"
IPA: /ɰa/

Trace and Practice

Variations

48

を
Wo
"O" as in "b<u>o</u>at"
IPA: /o/

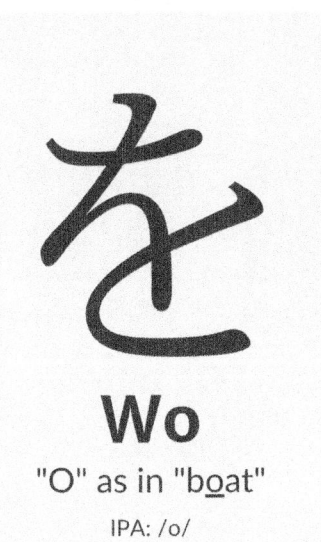

Stroke Order

Stroke Progression

Example Word

The hiragana character "を" is used exclusively as a particle.

In words, the sound "o" is written using the "お" character.

Trace and Practice

Variations

Stroke Order

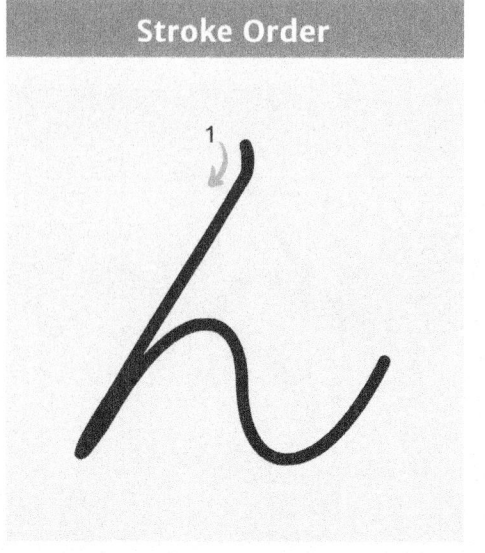

Stroke Progression

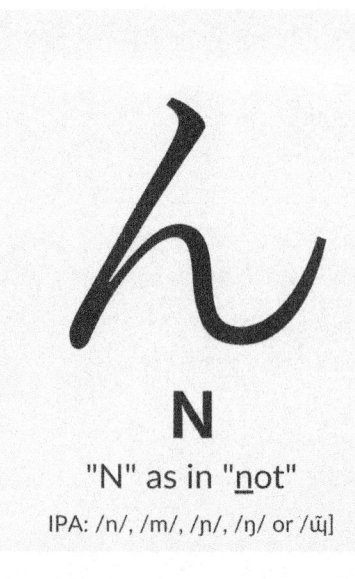

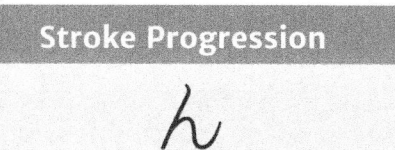

ん

Example Word

よん

Yon

Translation: Four

N

"N" as in "not"

IPA: /n/, /m/, /ɲ/, /ŋ/ or /ɰ̃]

Trace and Practice

Variations

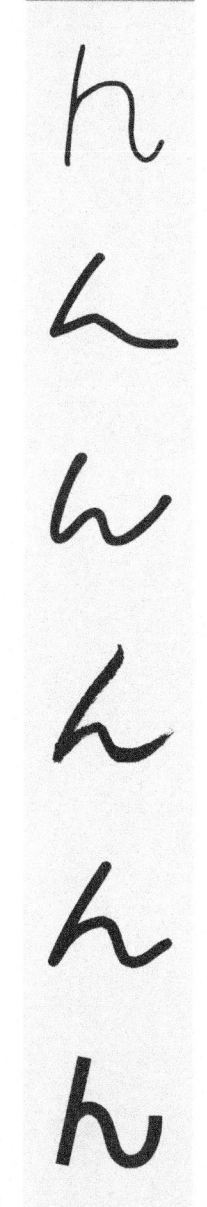

50

Sokuon

The syllable immediately after っ is duplicated but its vowel sound is removed. Effectively, this means doubling the consonant sound without doubling the vowel sound. At the end of a word in represents a glottal stop.

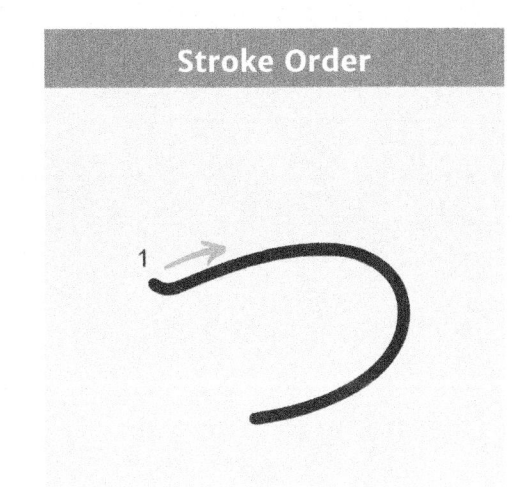

Stroke Order

Stroke Progression

っ

Example Word

いっしょ

Issho

Translation: Together / With

Trace and Practice

Variations

51

Bonus Training Page — Photocopy Me Freely

Bonus Training Page — Photocopy Me Freely

ア

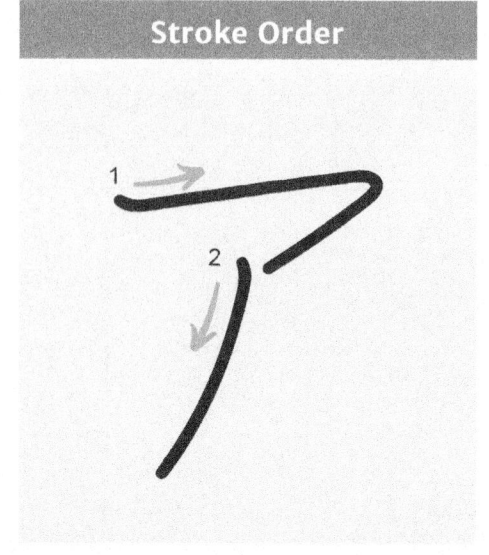

A

"A" as in "f<u>a</u>ther"

IPA: /a/

Stroke Order

Stroke Progression
フ ア

Example Word
アイデア

Aidea

Translation: Idea

Trace and Practice

Variations

54

イ

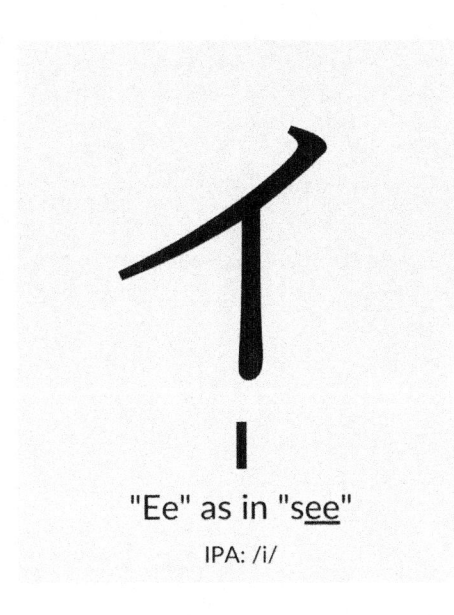

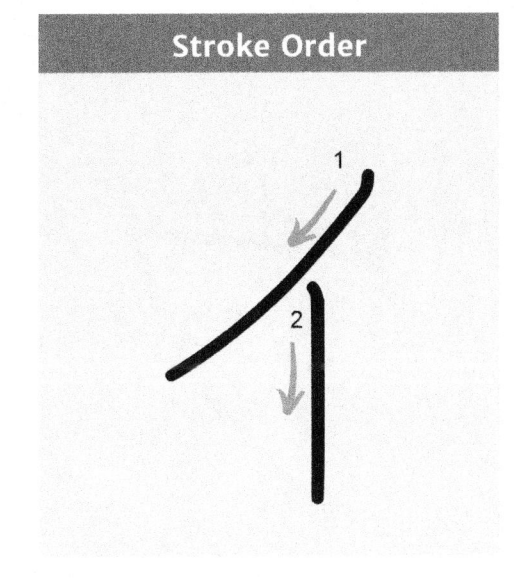

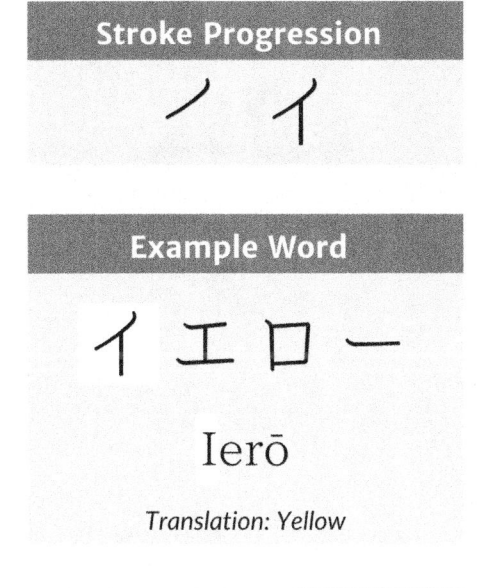

"Ee" as in "see"
IPA: /i/

Stroke Order

Stroke Progression
ノ イ

Example Word
イエロー

Ierō

Translation: Yellow

Trace and Practice

Variations

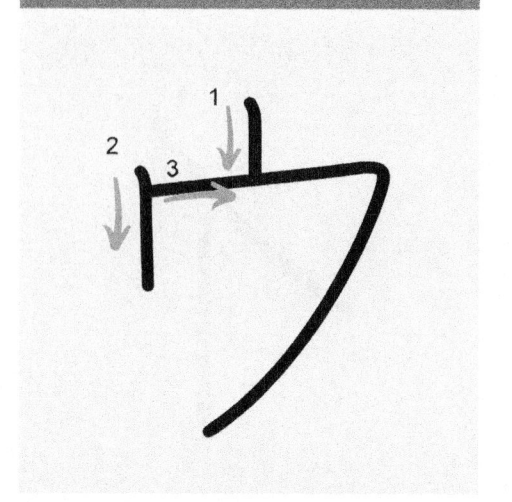

Stroke Order

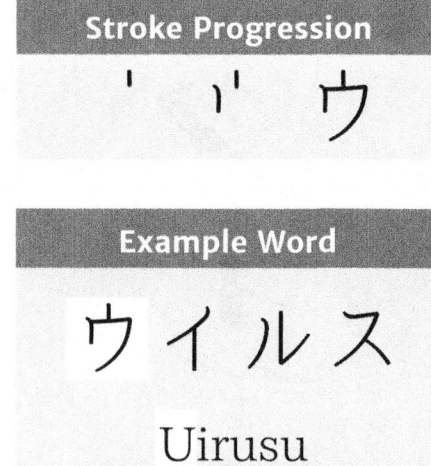

Stroke Progression

` ゛ ウ

Example Word

ウイルス

Uirusu

Translation: Virus

ウ
U
"Oo" as in "z<u>oo</u>"
IPA: /ɯ/

Trace and Practice

Variations

ウウウウウウ

Stroke Order

Stroke Progression

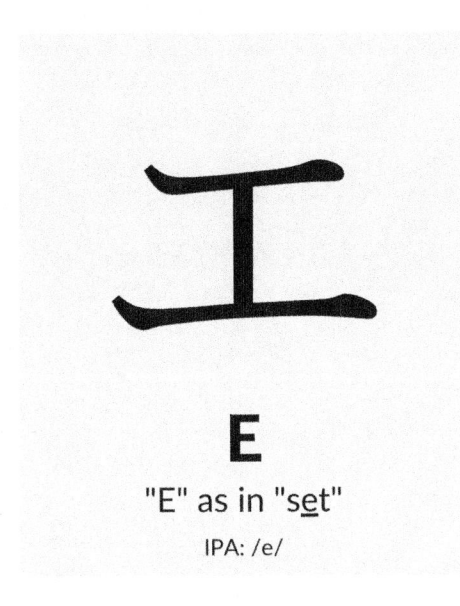

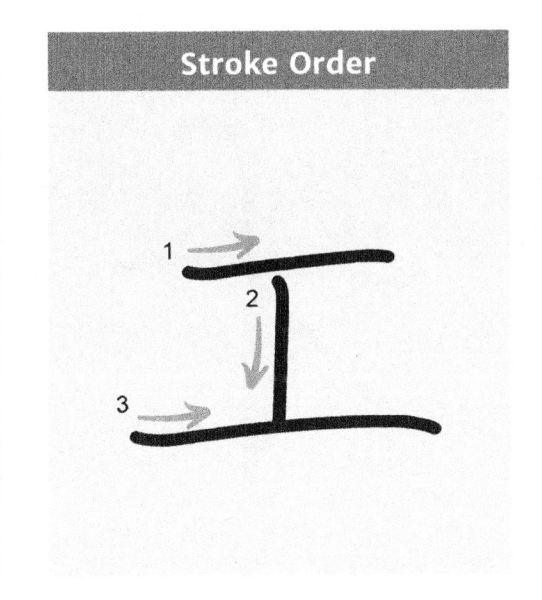

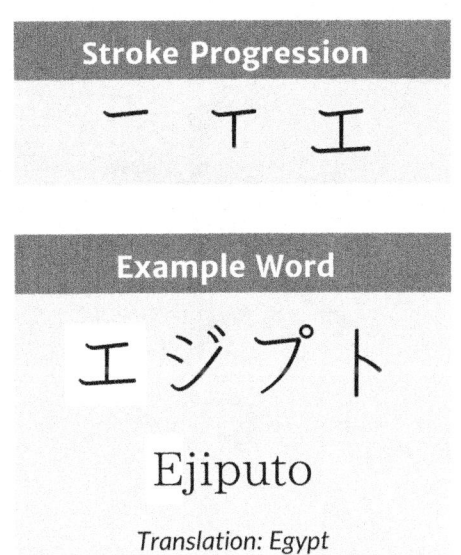

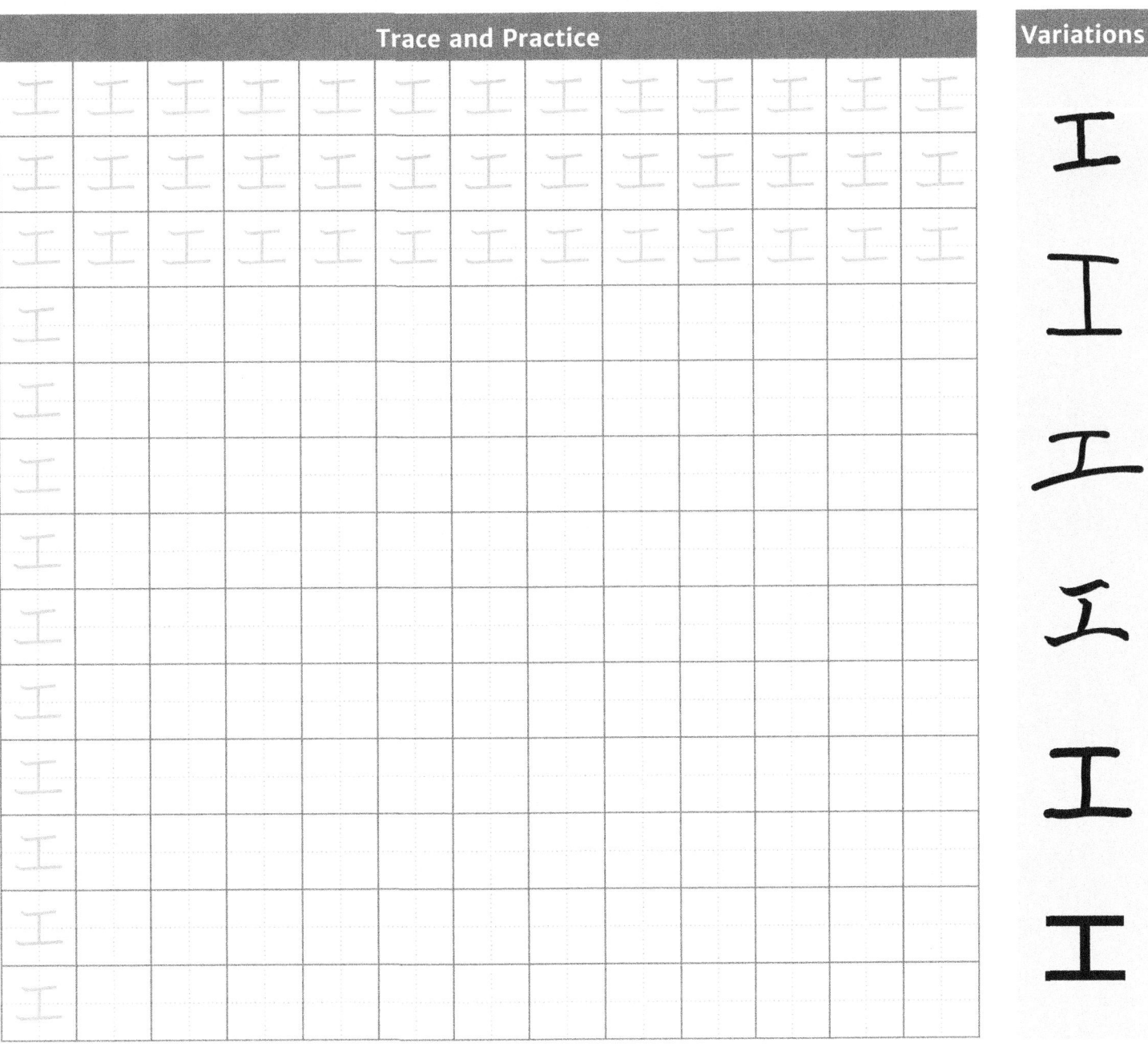

一 丁 エ

Example Word

エジプト

Ejiputo

Translation: Egypt

E

"E" as in "s<u>e</u>t"

IPA: /e/

Trace and Practice

Variations

57

Stroke Order

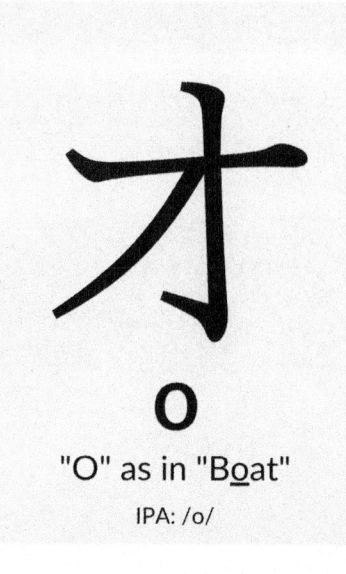

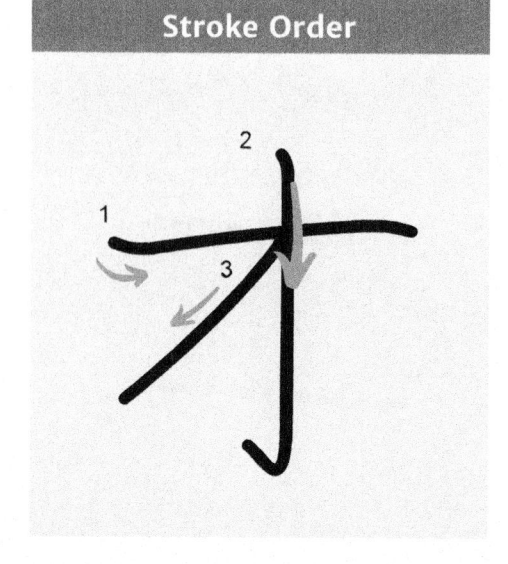

Stroke Progression
一 ナ オ

Example Word
オアシス

Oashisu

Translation: Oasis

オ
"O" as in "B<u>o</u>at"
IPA: /o/

Trace and Practice

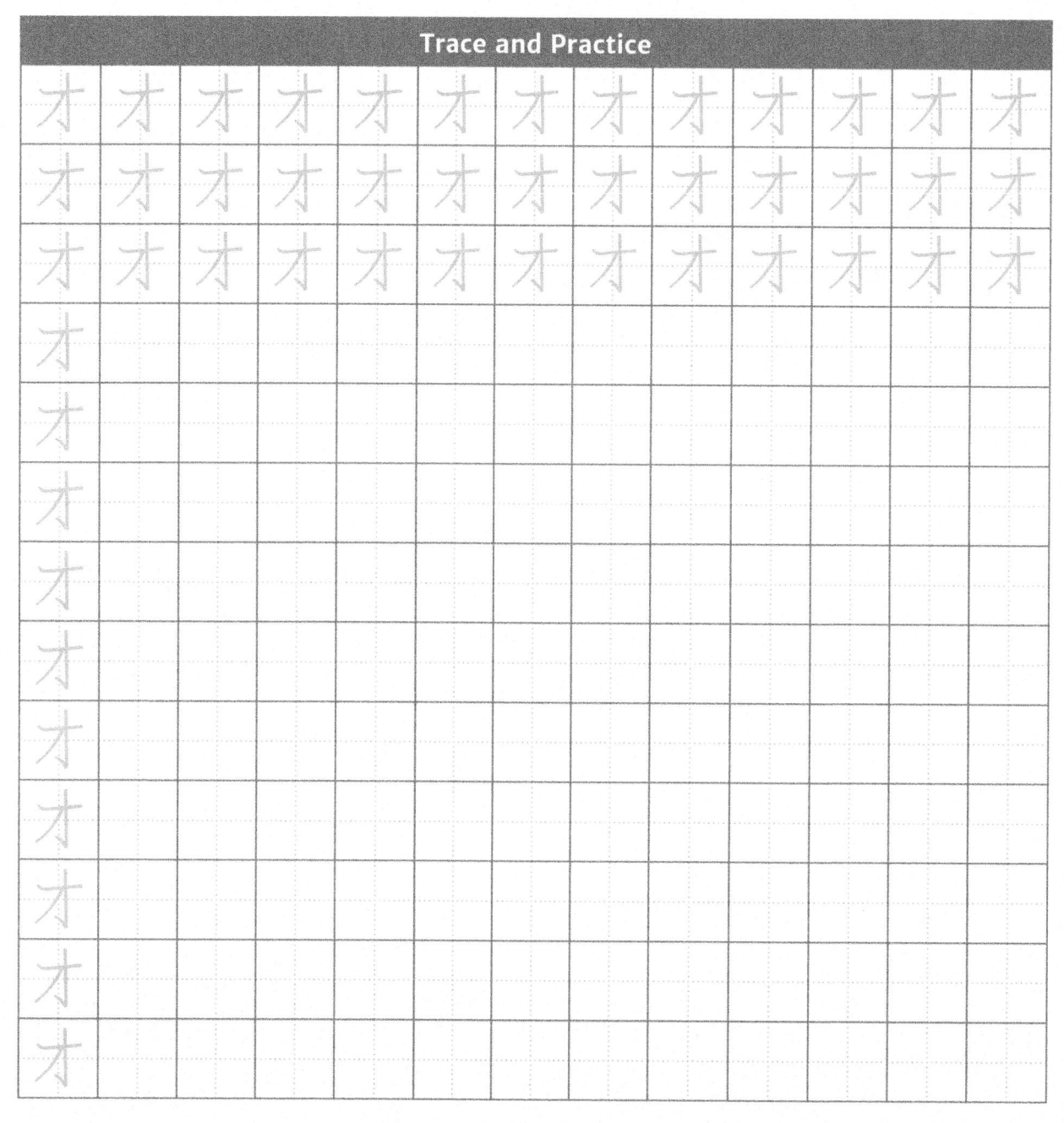

Variations

カ

Ka

"Ca" as in "cart"

IPA: /ka/

Stroke Order

Stroke Progression

マ カ

Example Word

カラフル

Karafuru

Translation: Colorful

Trace and Practice

Variations

Ki
"Key" as in "key"
IPA: /ki/

Stroke Order

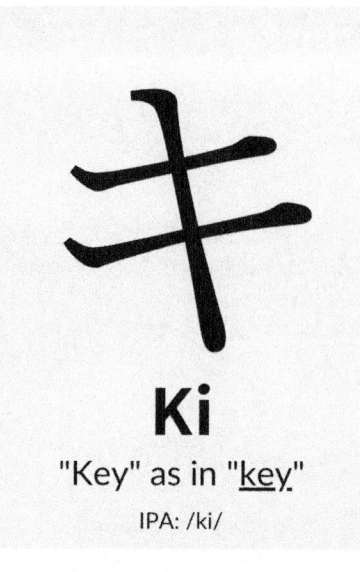

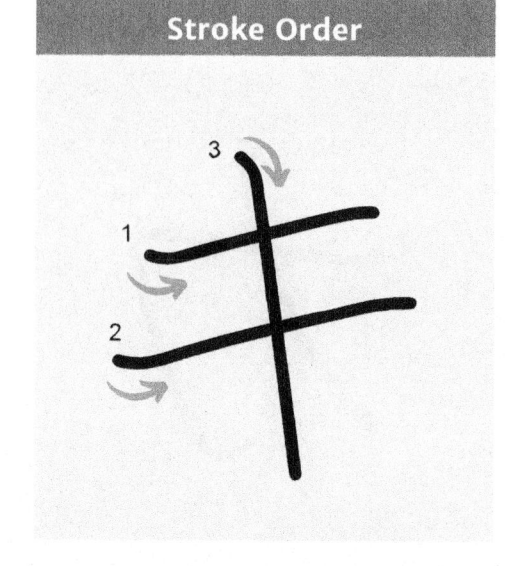

Stroke Progression
一 二 キ

Example Word
キオスク
Kiosuku
Translation: Kiosk

Trace and Practice

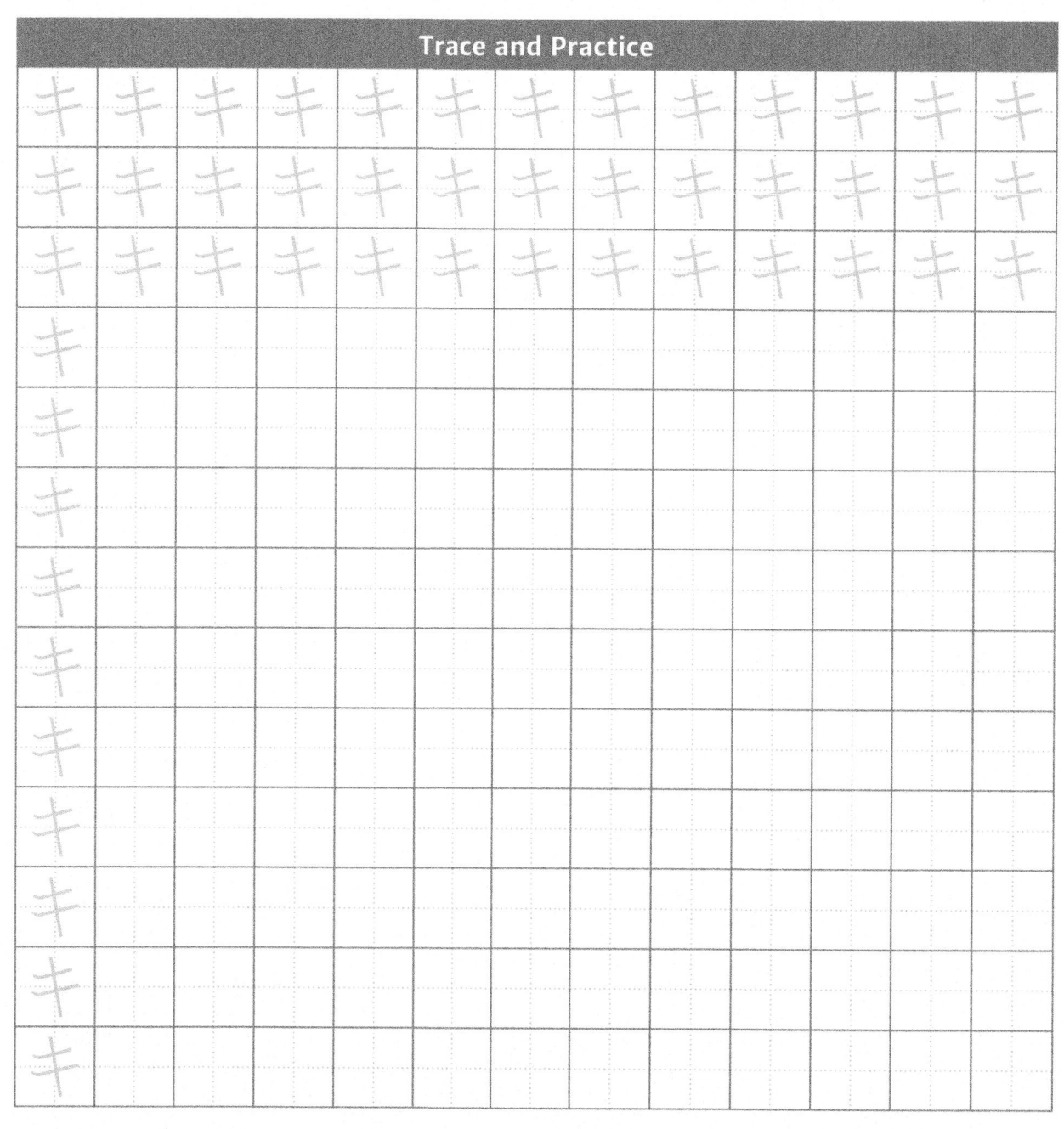

Variations

ク

Ku
"Coo" as in "cool"
IPA: /kɯ/

Stroke Order

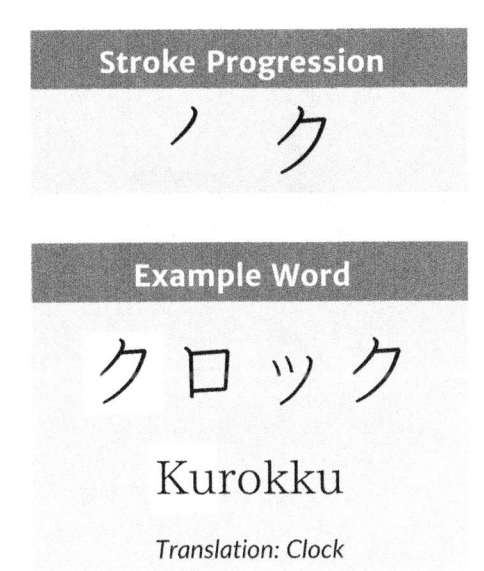

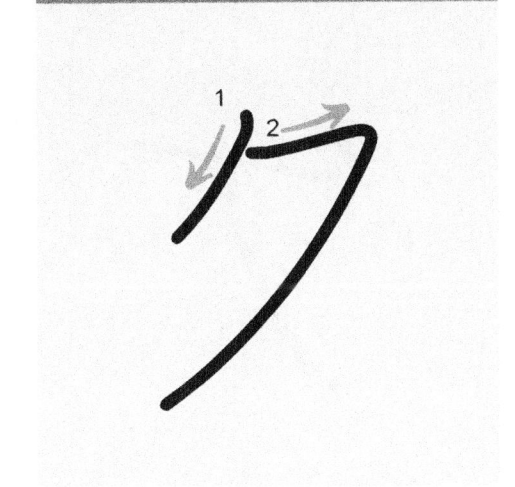

Stroke Progression
ノ ク

Example Word
クロック

Kurokku

Translation: Clock

Trace and Practice

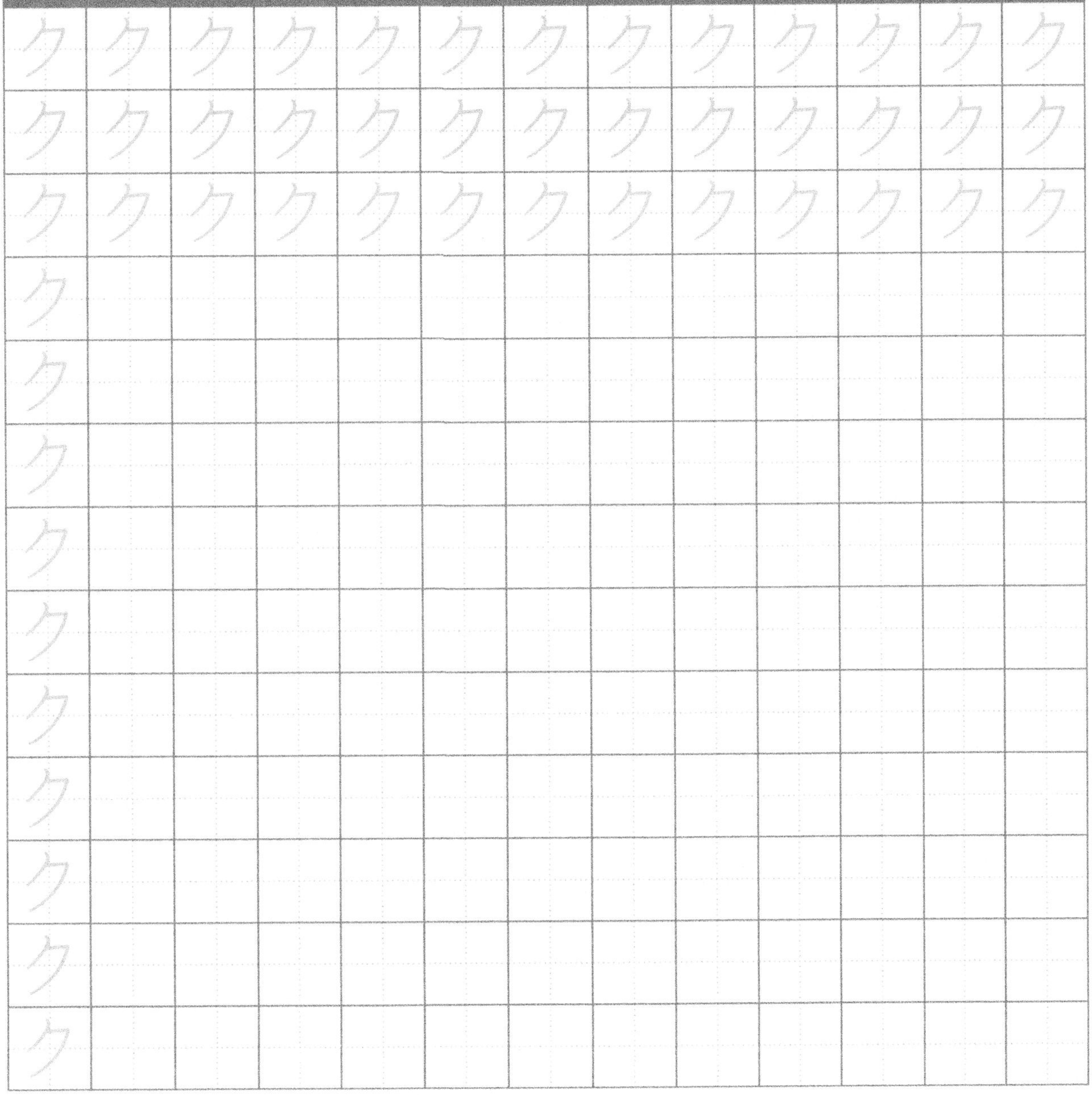

Variations

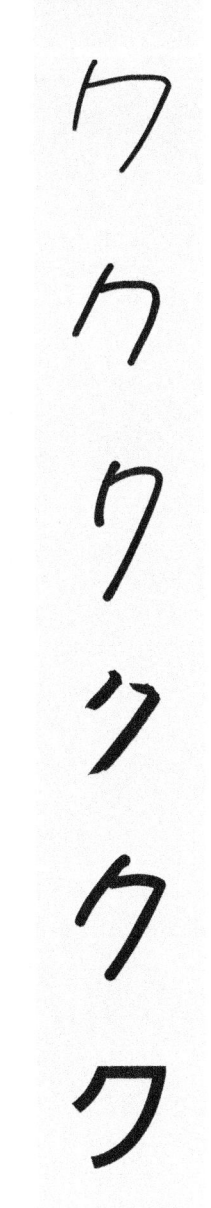

ケ

Ke
Similar to "Ke" as in "Kettle"
IPA: /ke/

Stroke Order

Stroke Progression

ノ 亻 ケ

Example Word

ケーブル

Kēburu

Translation: Cable

Trace and Practice

Variations

Stroke Order

Stroke Progression

ヿ コ

Example Word

コングラ

Kongura

Translation: Congratulations

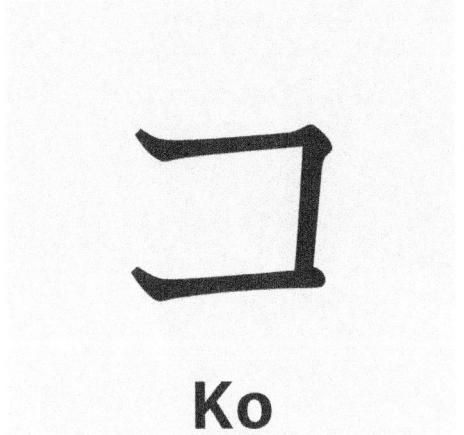

Ko

Similar to "ko" as in "<u>Ko</u>rea"

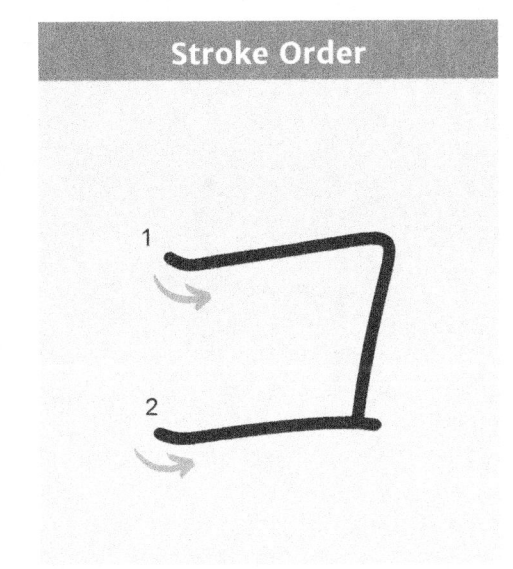

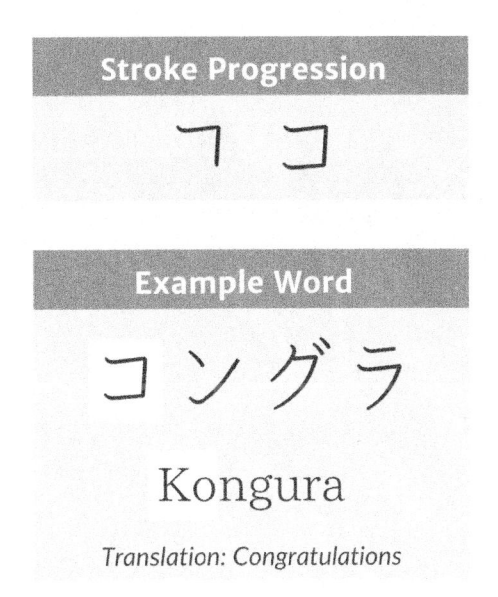

IPA: /ko/

Trace and Practice

Variations

サ
Sa
"Sa" as in "salsa"
IPA: /sa/

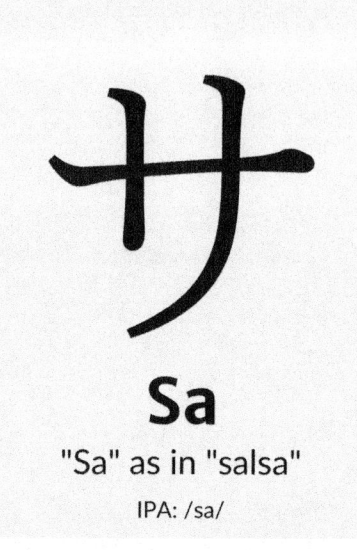

Stroke Order

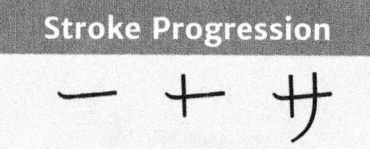

Stroke Progression
一 十 サ

Example Word
サイクル
Saikuru
Translation: Cycle / Bicycle

Trace and Practice

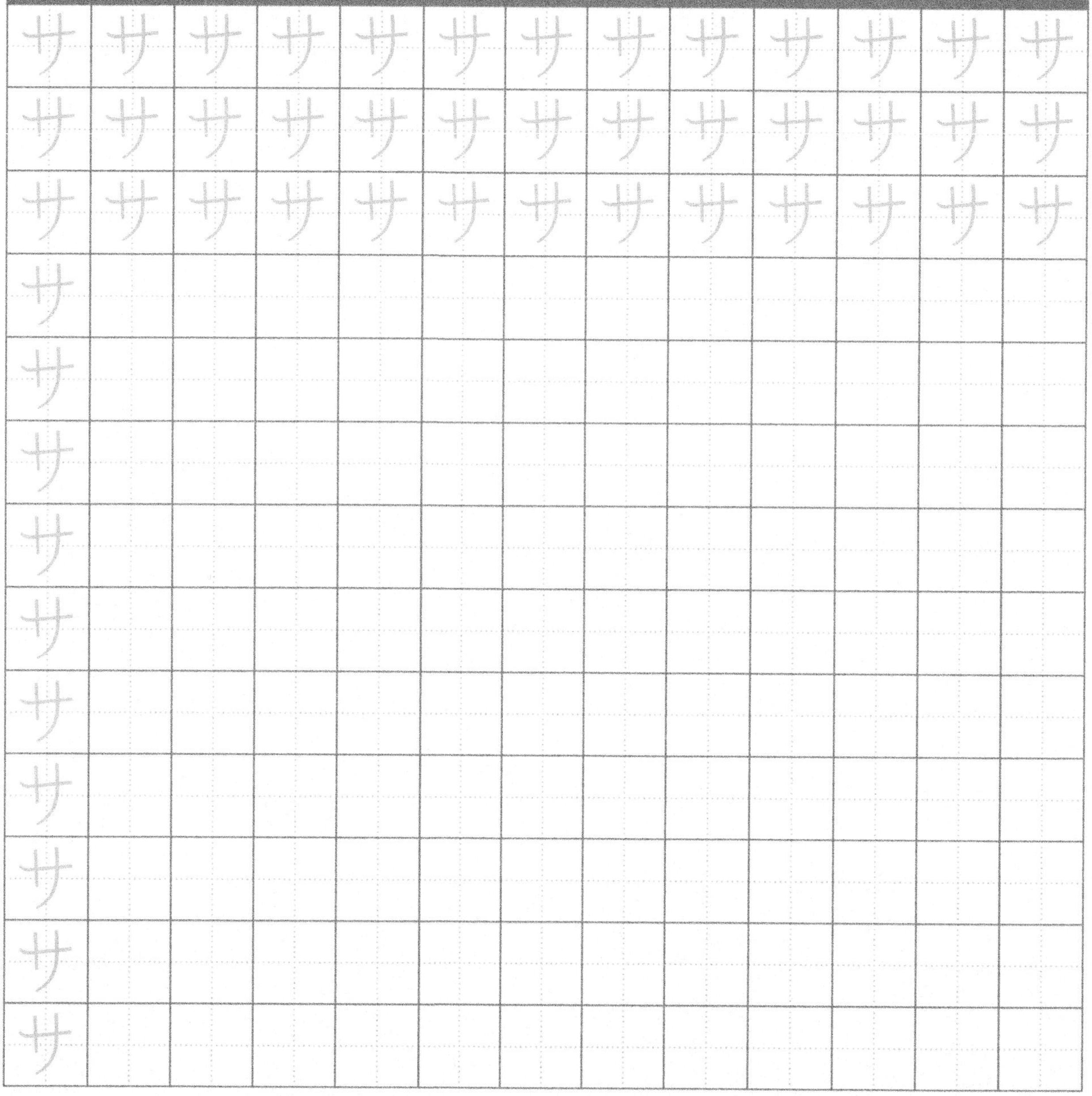

Variations

Shi

"She" as in "she"

IPA: /ɕi/

Stroke Order

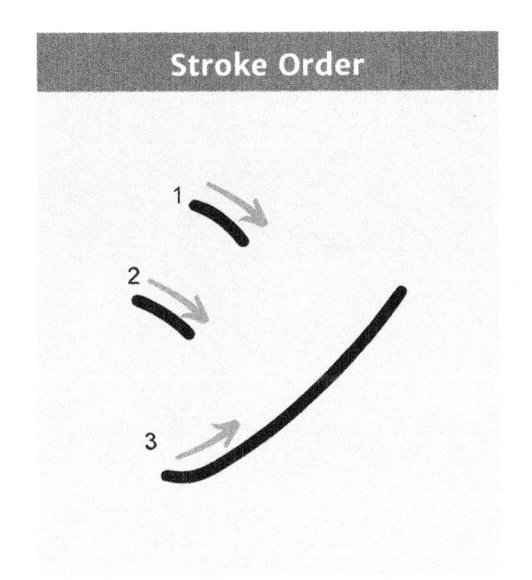

Stroke Progression

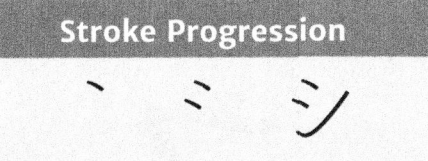

Example Word

シンプル

Shipuru

Translation: Simple

Trace and Practice

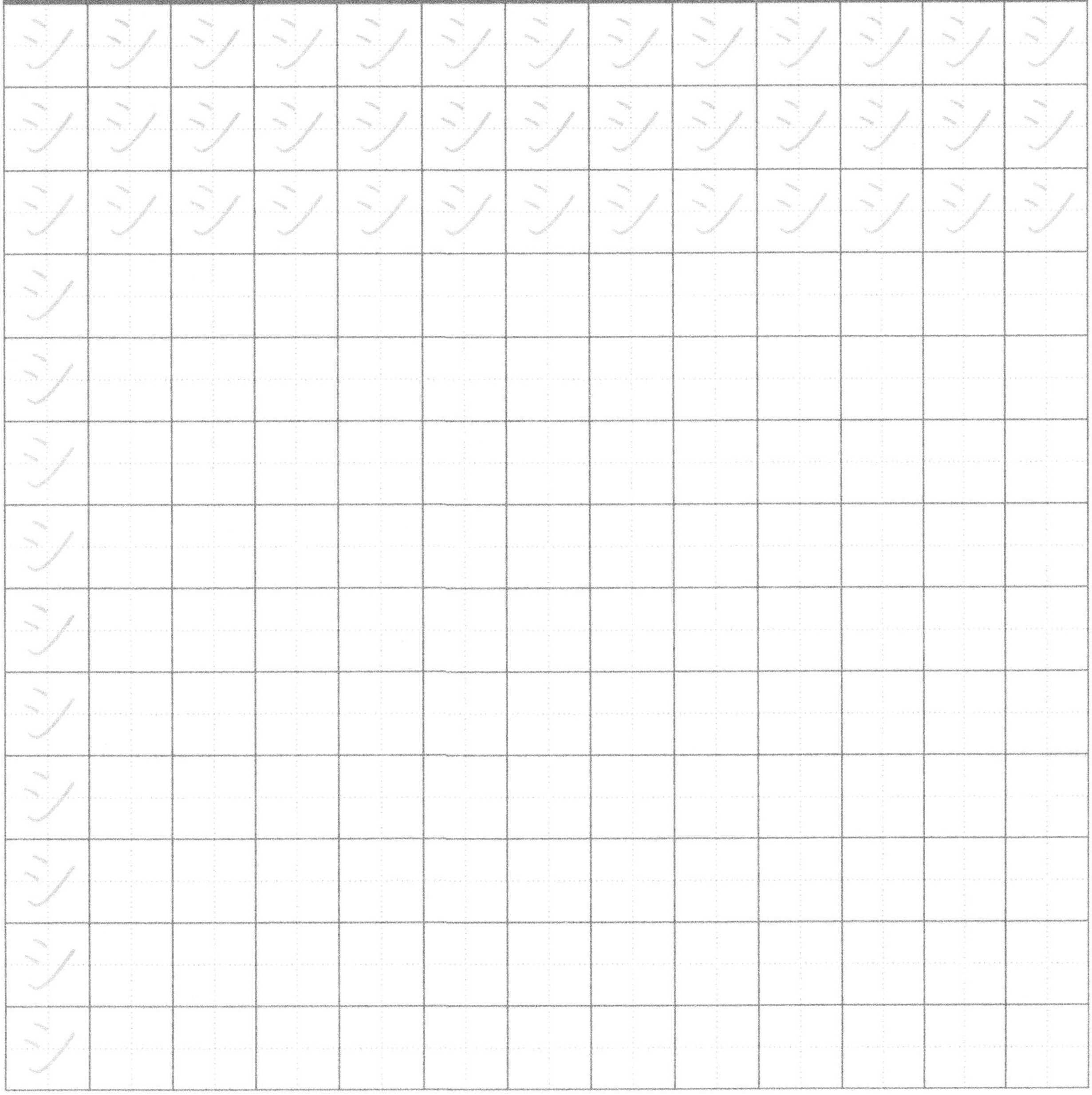

Variations

Su

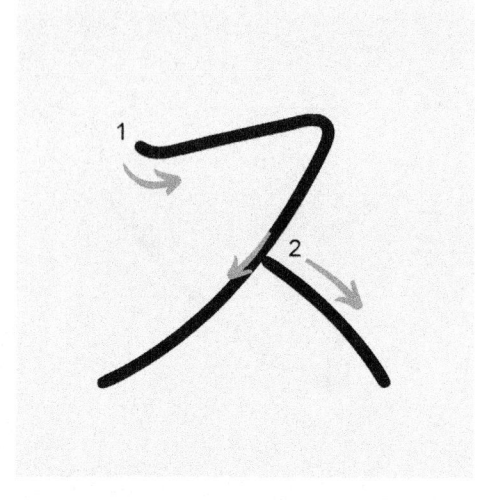

ス

"Su" as in "suchi"

IPA: /sɯ/

Stroke Order

Stroke Progression

フ ス

Example Word

ス ピーチ

Supīchi

Translation: A speech / A talk

Trace and Practice

Variations

ス ス ス ス ス ス ス ス

セ

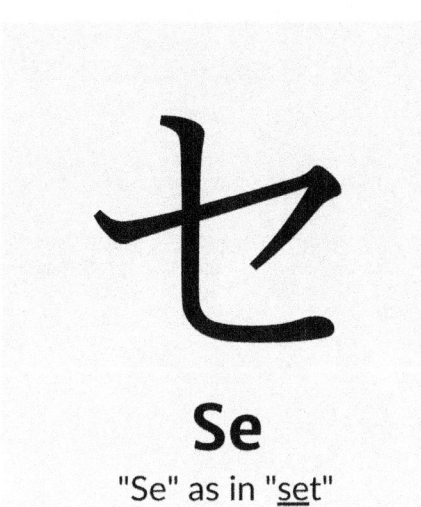

Se

"Se" as in "set"

IPA: /se/

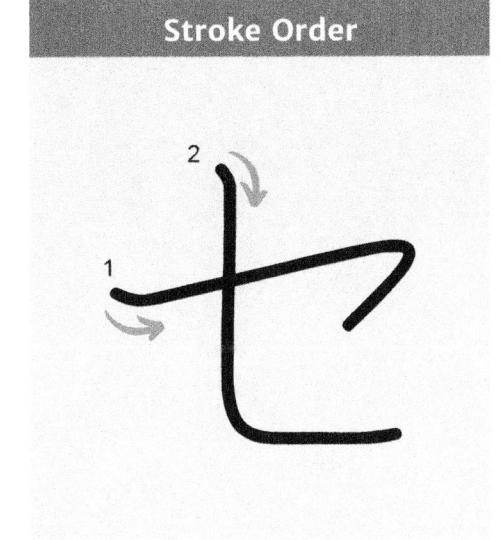

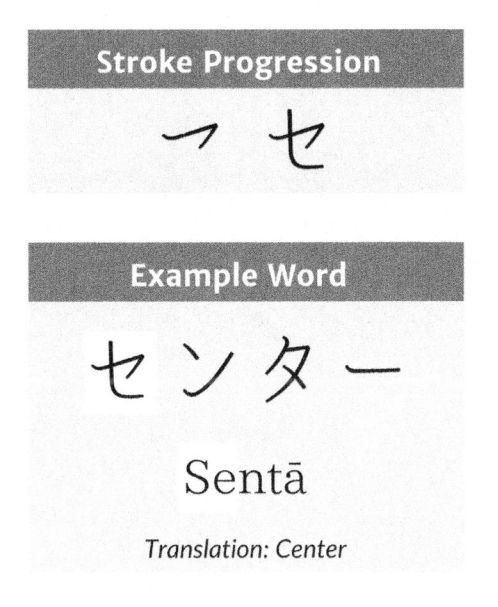

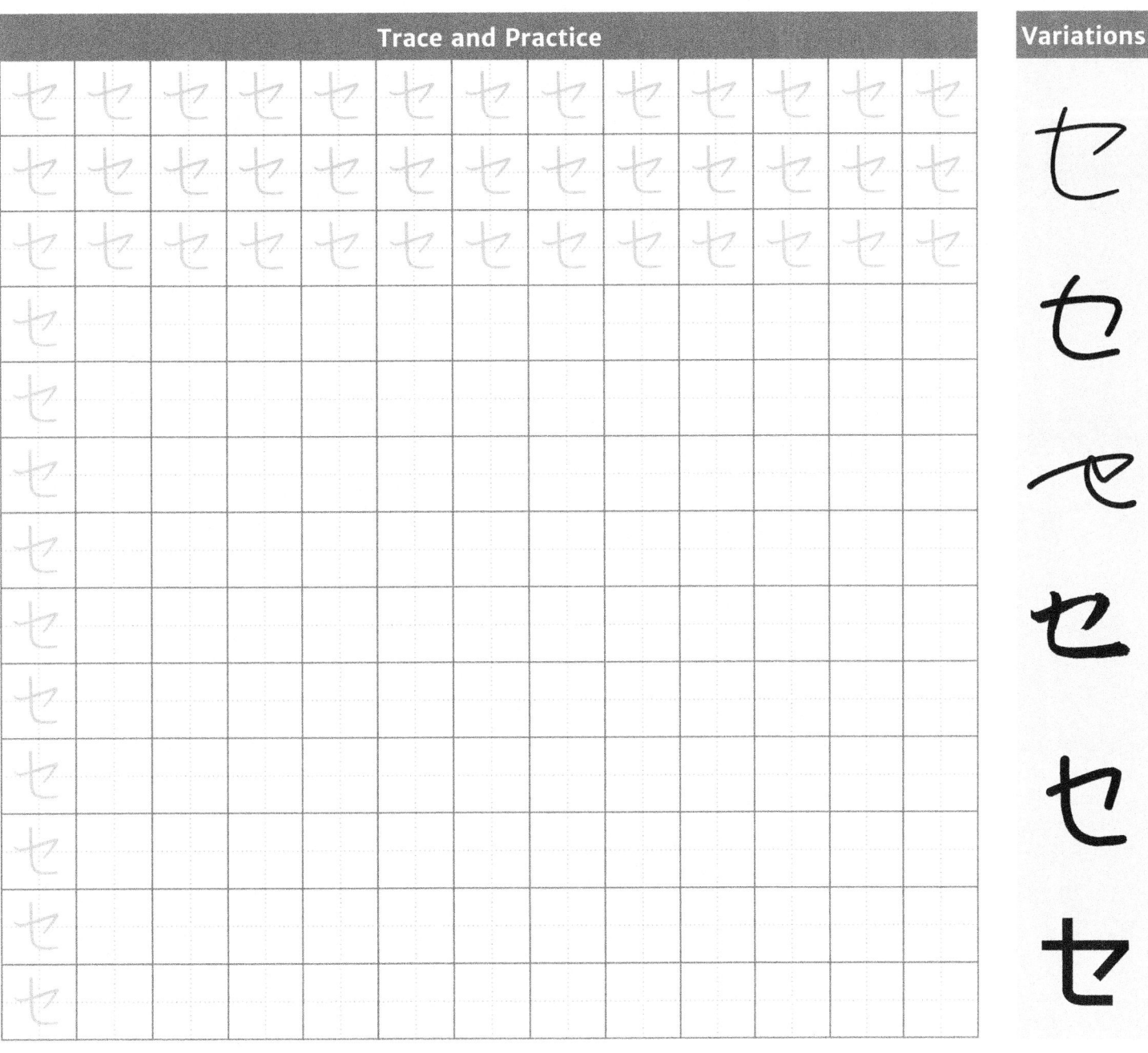

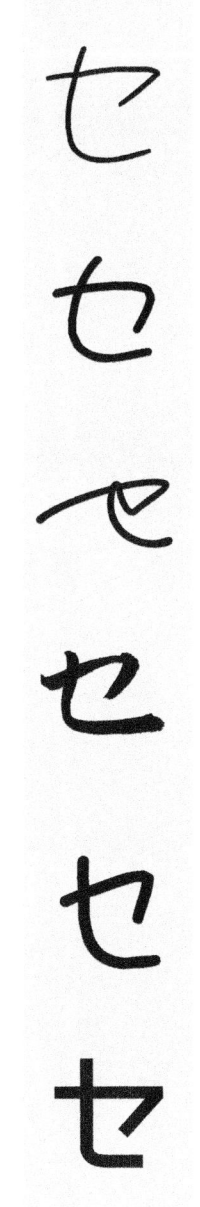

Stroke Order

Stroke Progression

Example Word

センター

Sentā

Translation: Center

Trace and Practice

Variations

ソ

So

"So" as in "<u>so</u>"

IPA: /so/

Stroke Order

Stroke Progression

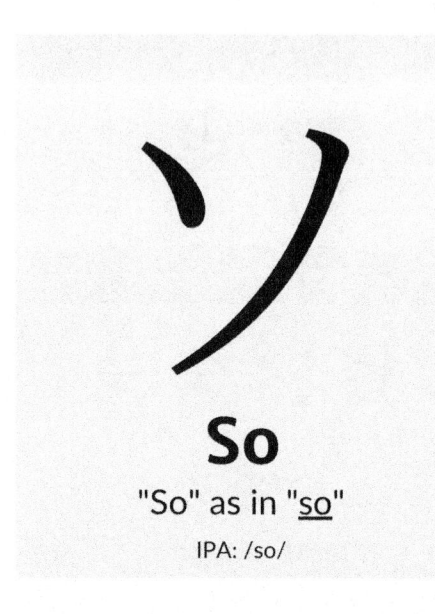

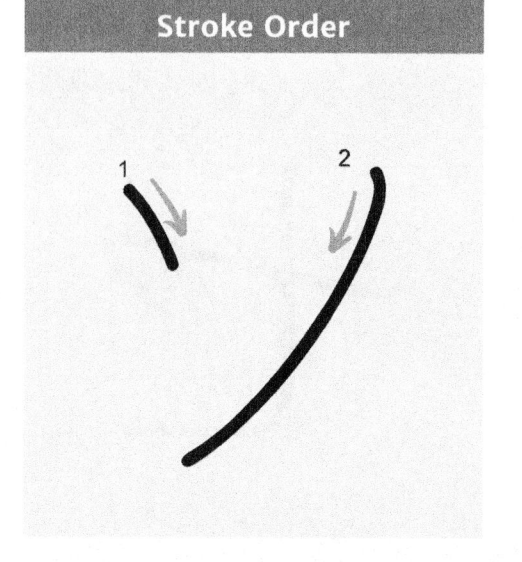

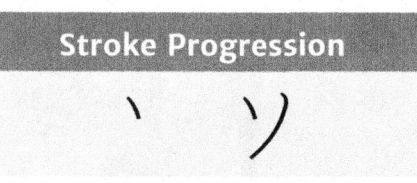

ヽ ソ

Example Word

ソックス

Sokkusu

Translation: Socks

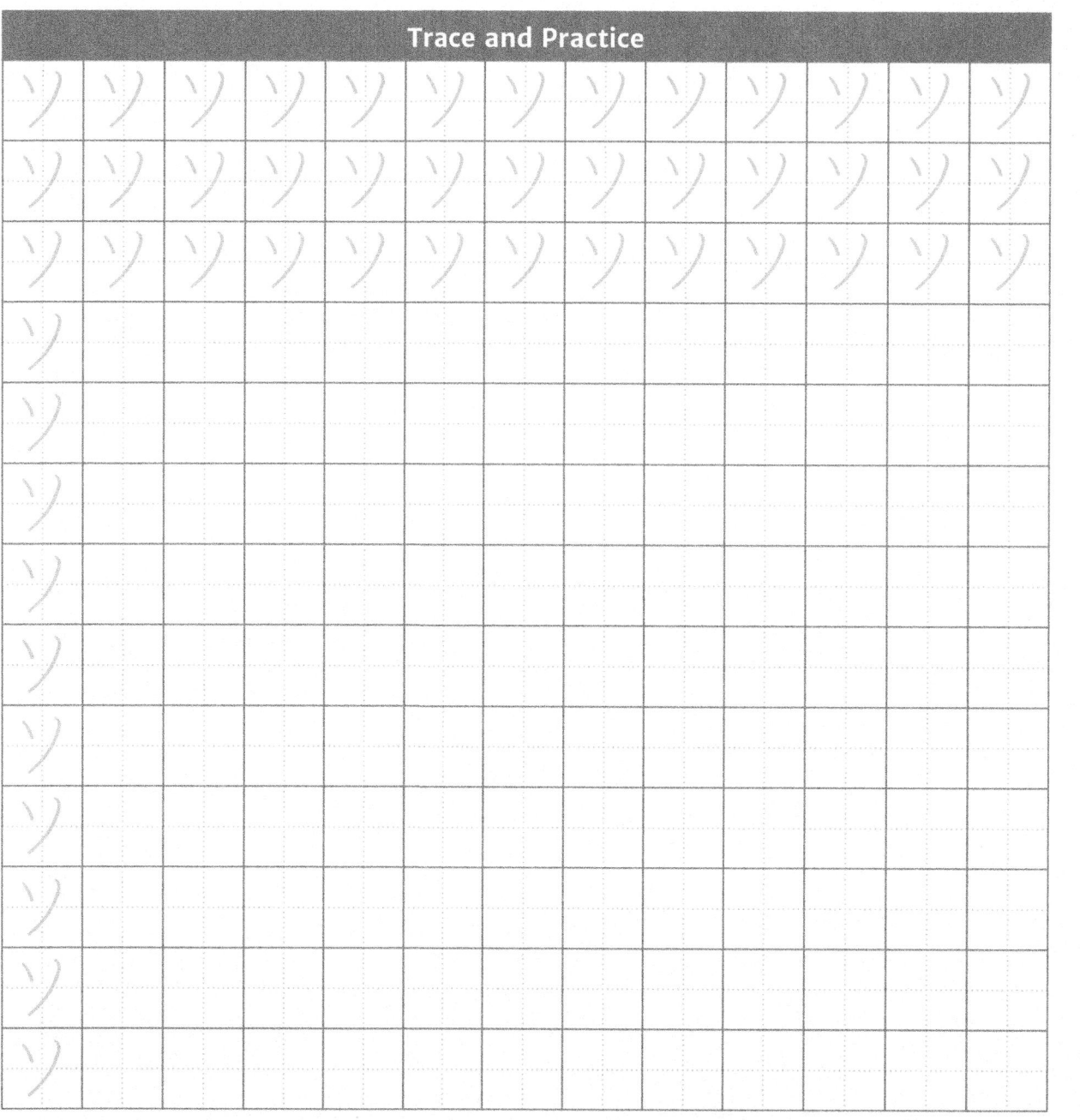

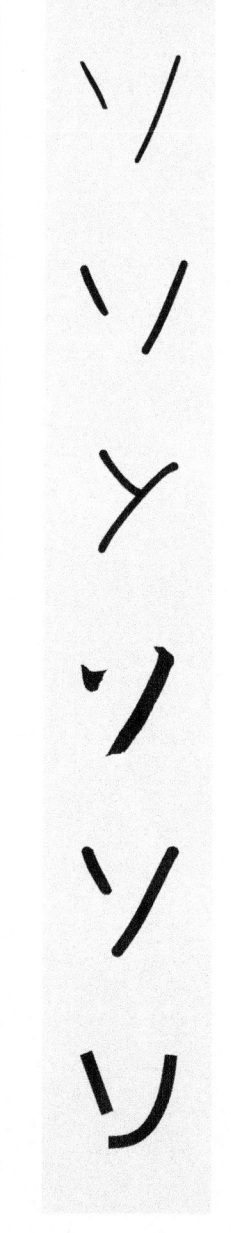

Trace and Practice

Variations

68

Ta

タ

"Ta" as in "tall"

IPA: /ta/

Stroke Order

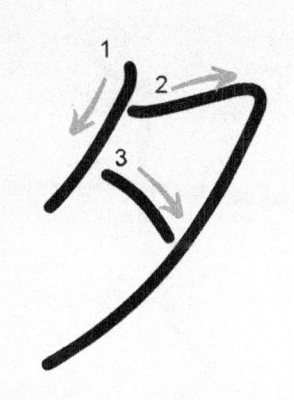

Stroke Progression

ノ　ク　タ

Example Word

タクシー

Takushī

Translation: Taxi

Trace and Practice

Variations

Chi
"Chea" as in "cheat"
IPA: /tɕi/

Stroke Order

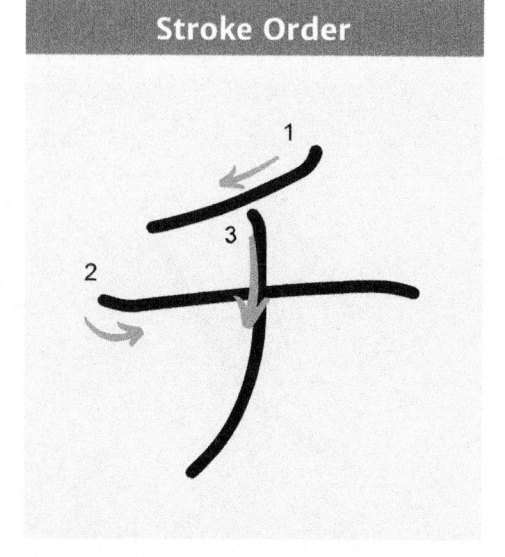

Stroke Progression
ノ 二 チ

Example Word
チケット
Chiketto
Translation: Ticket

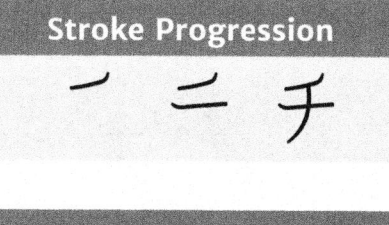

Trace and Practice

Variations

ツ

Tsu

"Tsu" as in "tsunami"

IPA: /tsɯ/

Stroke Order

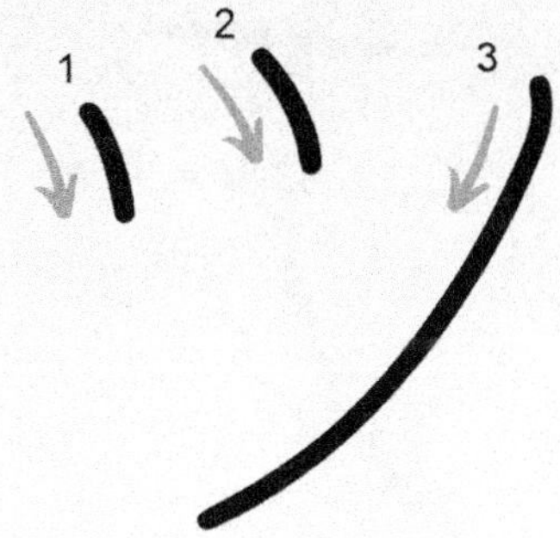

Stroke Progression

ヽ　ヾ　ツ

Example Word

ツイスト

Tsuīto

Translation: Tweet (on Twitter)

Trace and Practice

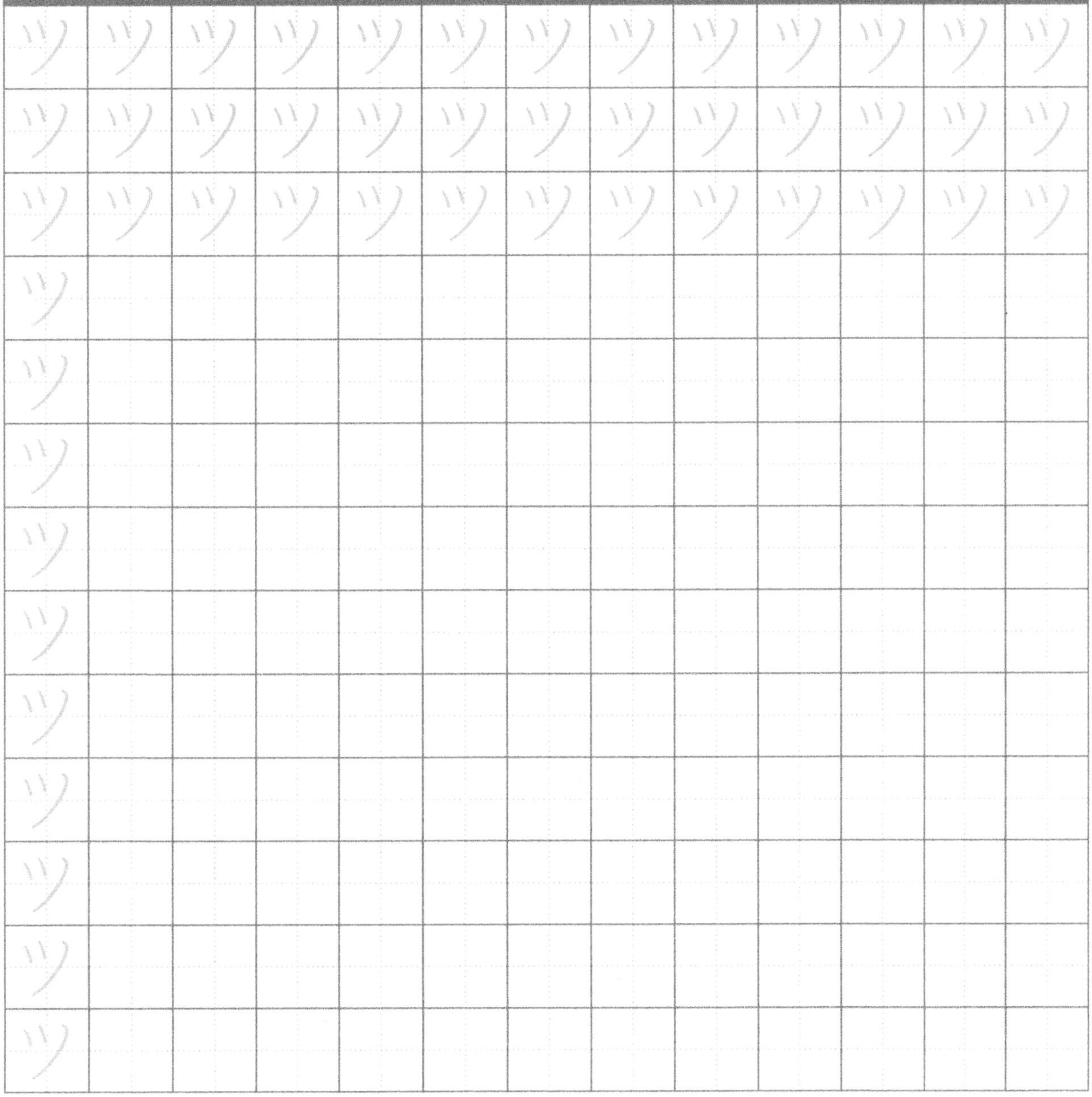

Variations

71

テ
Te
"Te" as in "test"
IPA: /te/

Stroke Order

Stroke Progression
一 二 テ

Example Word
テキスト
Tekisuto
Translation: Text

Trace and Practice

Variations

To

ト

"To" as in "<u>to</u>ad"

IPA: /to/

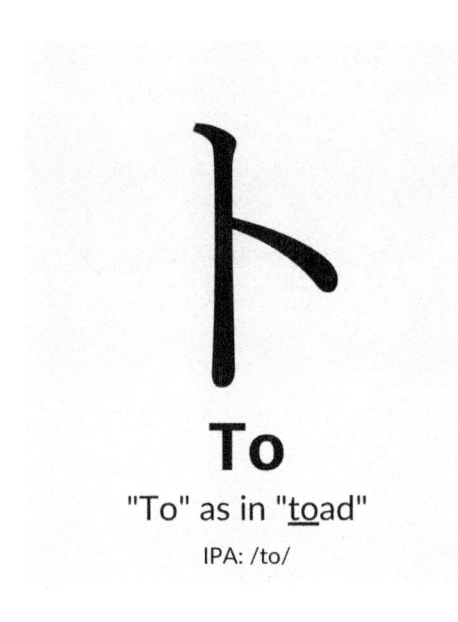

Stroke Order

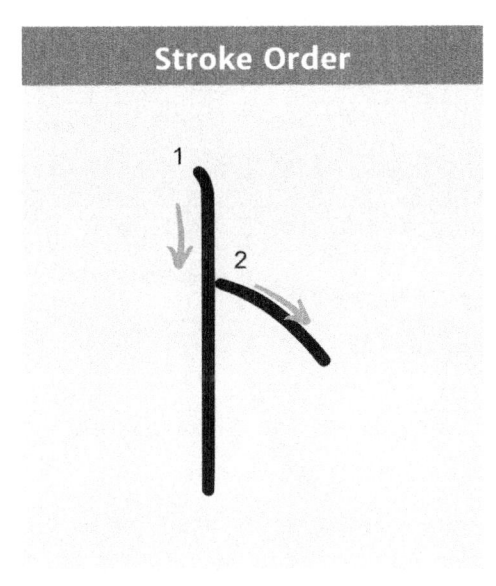

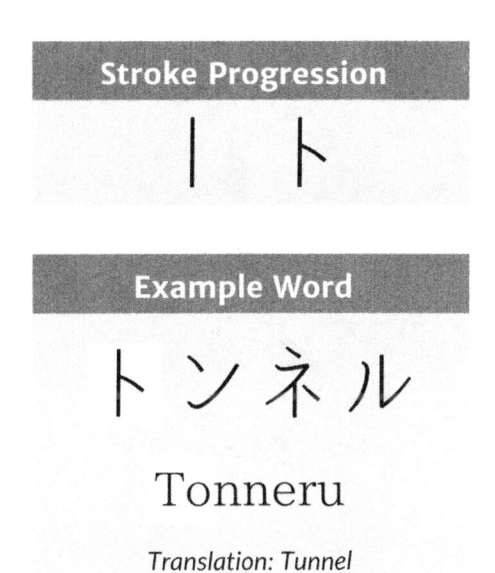

Stroke Progression

Ｉ ト

Example Word

トンネル

Tonneru

Translation: Tunnel

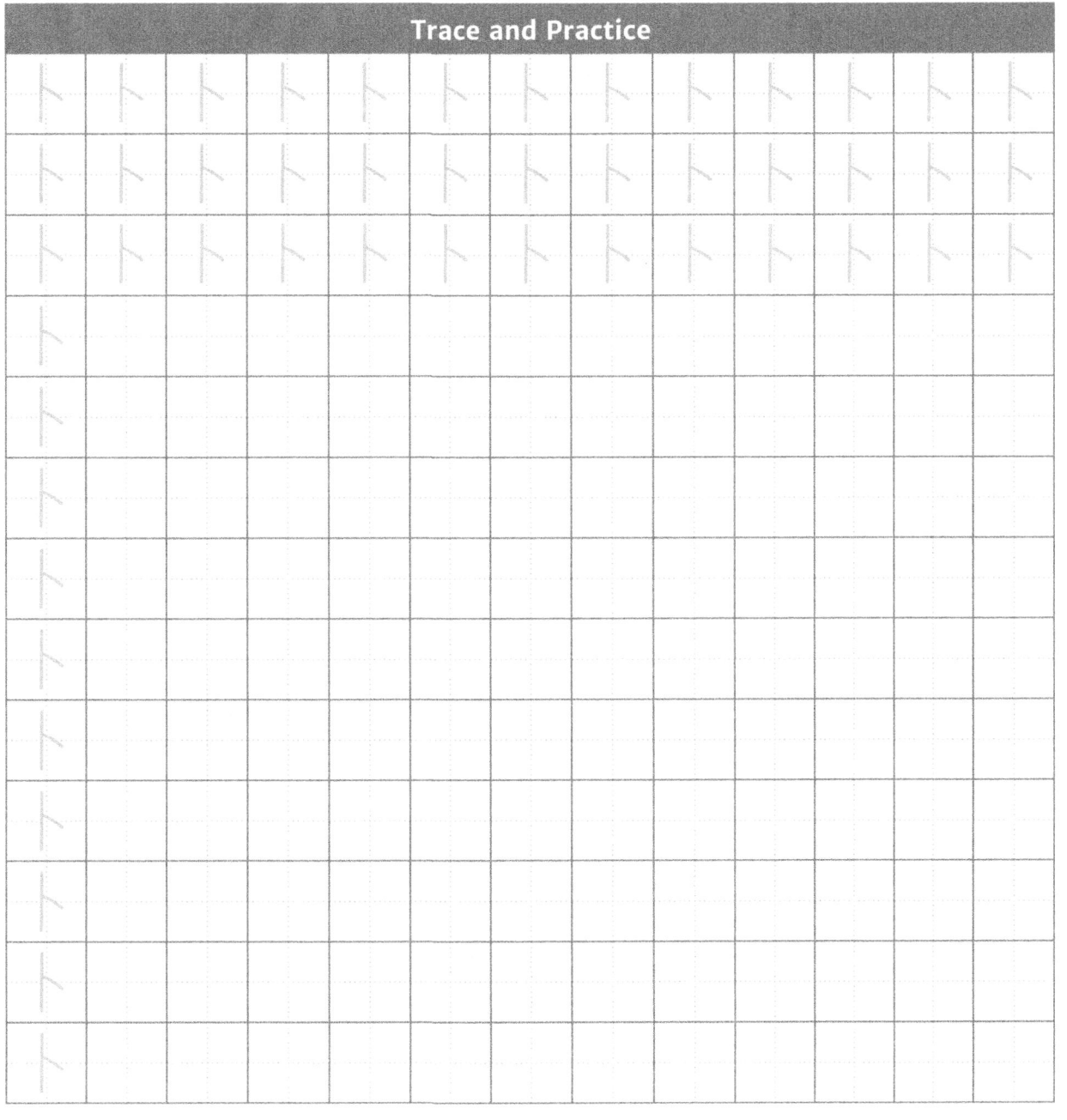

Trace and Practice

Variations

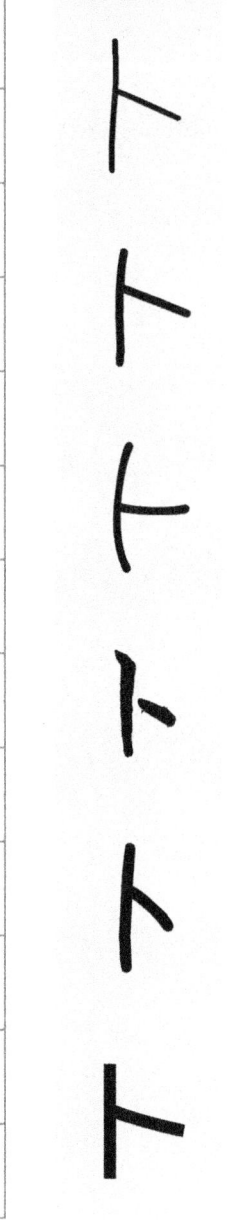

ト
ト
ト
ト
ト
ト
ト

ナ
Na
"Na" as in "nacho"
IPA: /na/

Stroke Order

Stroke Progression
一 ナ

Example Word
ナプキン
Napukin
Translation: Napkin

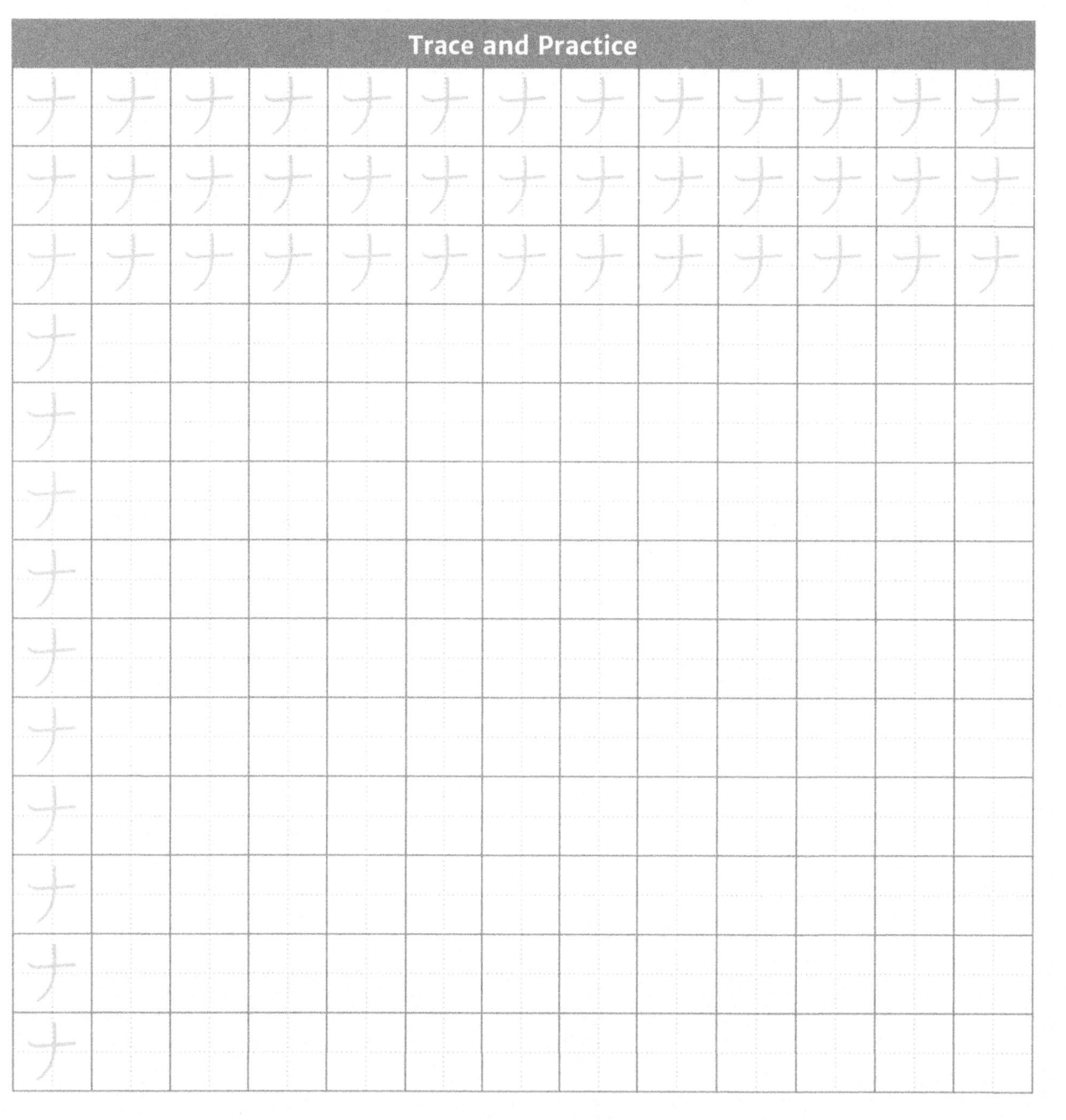

Trace and Practice

Variations

Ni
"Knee" as in "Knee"
IPA: /ɲi/

Stroke Order

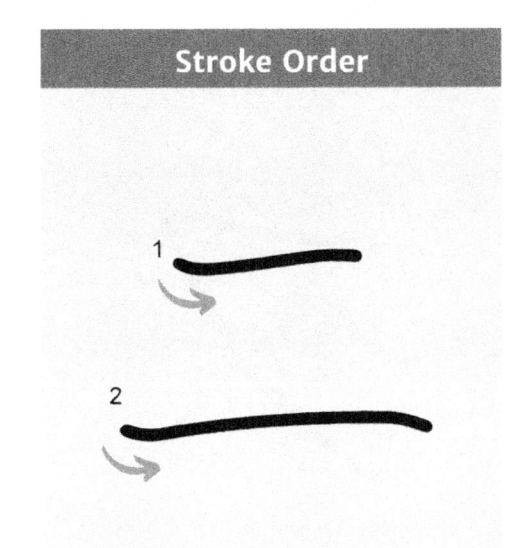

Stroke Progression

Example Word

Nikoniko

Translation: Smile

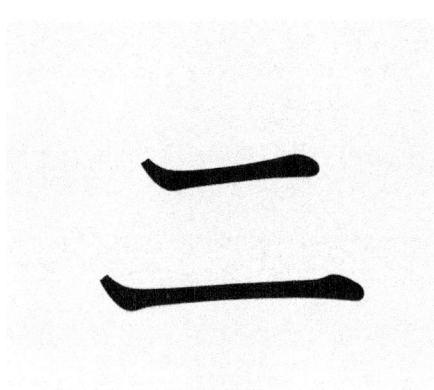

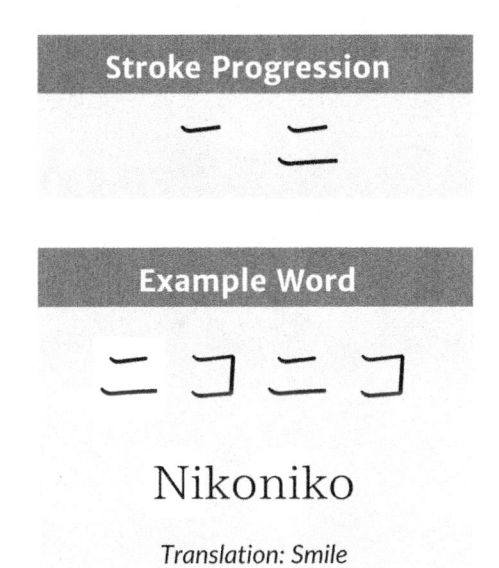

Trace and Practice

Variations

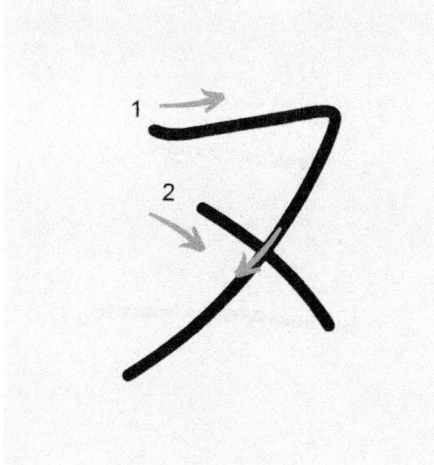

Stroke Order

Stroke Progression

フ ヌ

ヌ

Nu
"Knew" as in "knew"
IPA: /nɯ/

Example Word

ヌードル

Nūdoru

Translation: Noodle

Trace and Practice

Variations

76

Ne

"Ne" as in "Net"

IPA: /ne/

Stroke Order

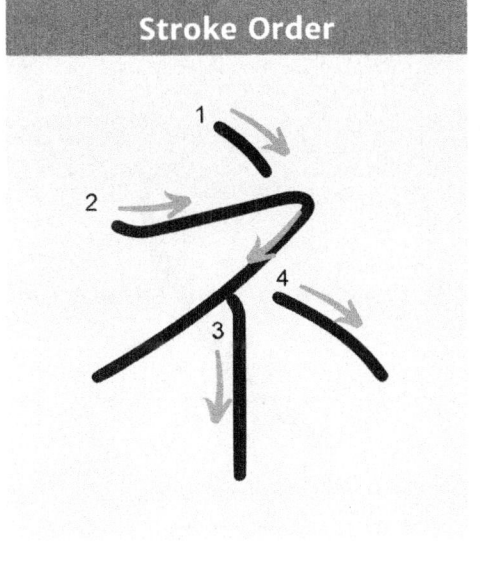

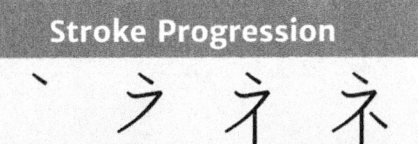

Stroke Progression

丶 ラ ネ ネ

Example Word

ネバネバ

Nebaneba

Translation: Persistence / Sticky

Trace and Practice

Variations

ネネネネネネ

No
"No" as in "No"
IPA: /no/

Stroke Order

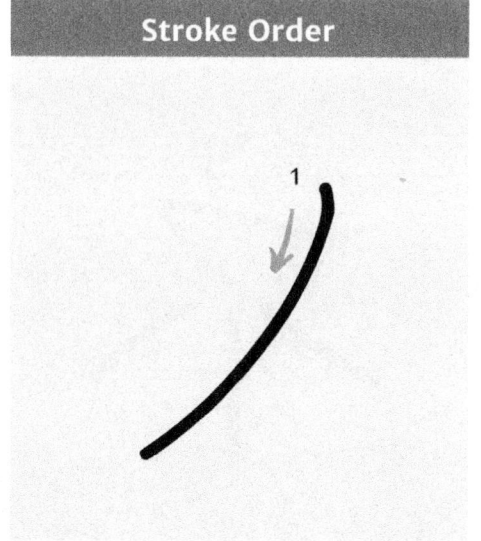

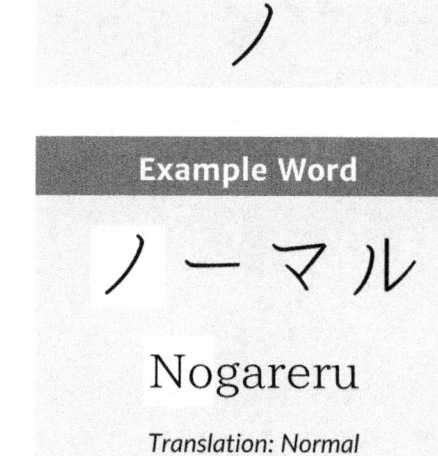

Stroke Progression

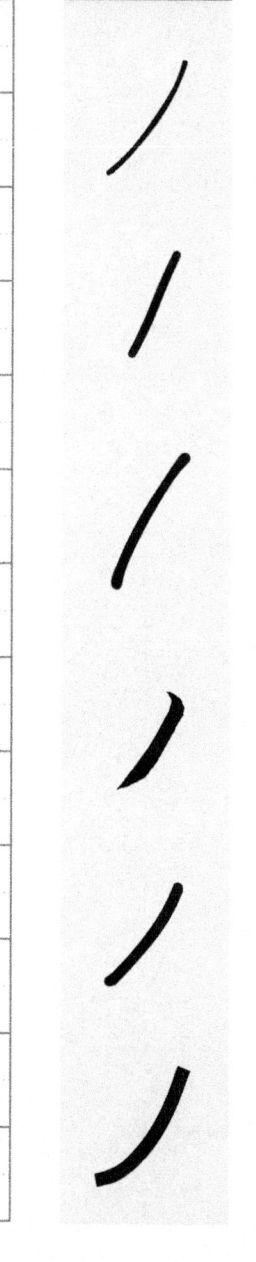

Example Word
ノーマル
Nogareru
Translation: Normal

Trace and Practice

Variations

78

Ha

ハ

"Ha" as in "haul"

IPA: /ha/, /ɯa/ as particle

Stroke Order

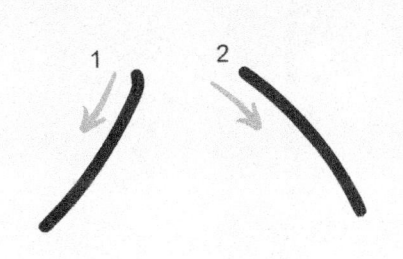

1 ノ 2 ハ

Stroke Progression

ノ ハ

Example Word

ハッピー

Happī

Translation: Happy

Trace and Practice

Variations

ハ ハ ハ ハ ハ ハ

Hi
"He" as in "he"
IPA: /çi/

Stroke Order
ヒ

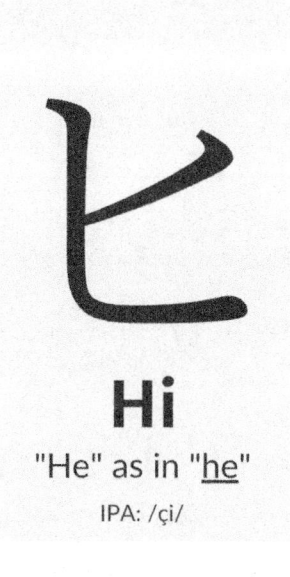

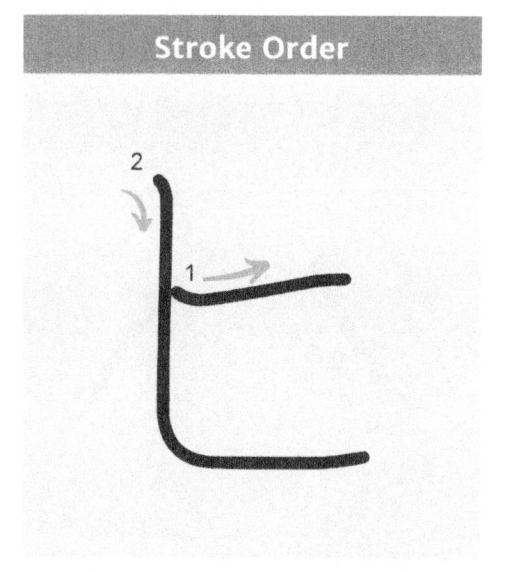

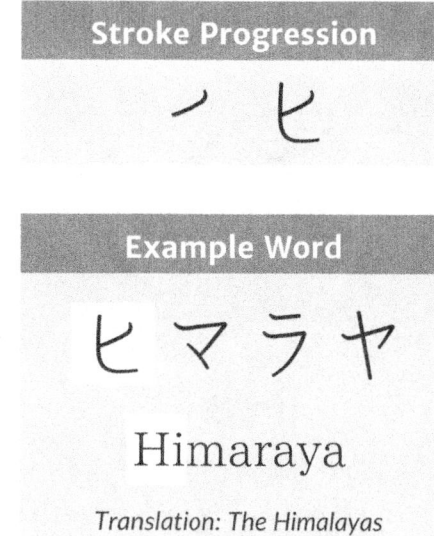

Stroke Progression
ノ ヒ

Example Word
ヒマラヤ

Himaraya

Translation: The Himalayas

Trace and Practice

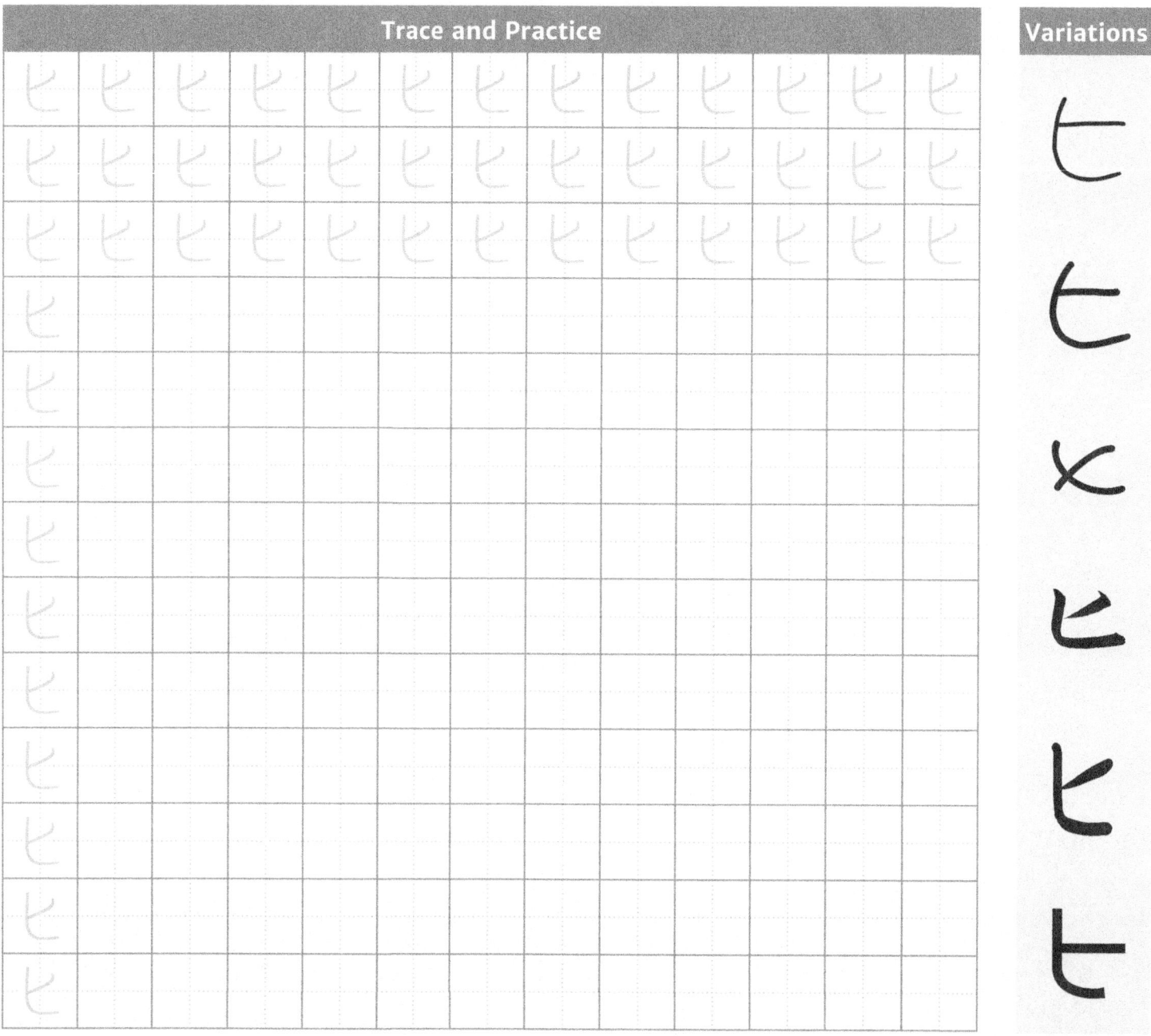

Variations
ヒ ヒ ヒ ㄨ ヒ ヒ ヒ ヒ

80

フ
Fu
"Foo" as in "Fool"
IPA: /ɸɯ/

Stroke Order

Stroke Progression
フ

Example Word
フィルム
Firumu
Translation: Cinema / Camera film

Trace and Practice

Variations

He

"He" as in "Head"

IPA: /he/, /e/ as a particle

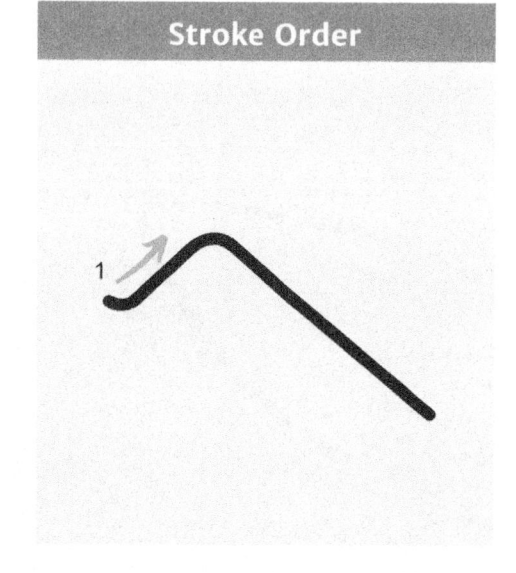

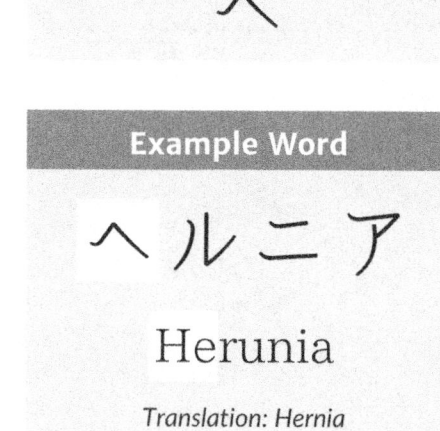

Stroke Order

Stroke Progression

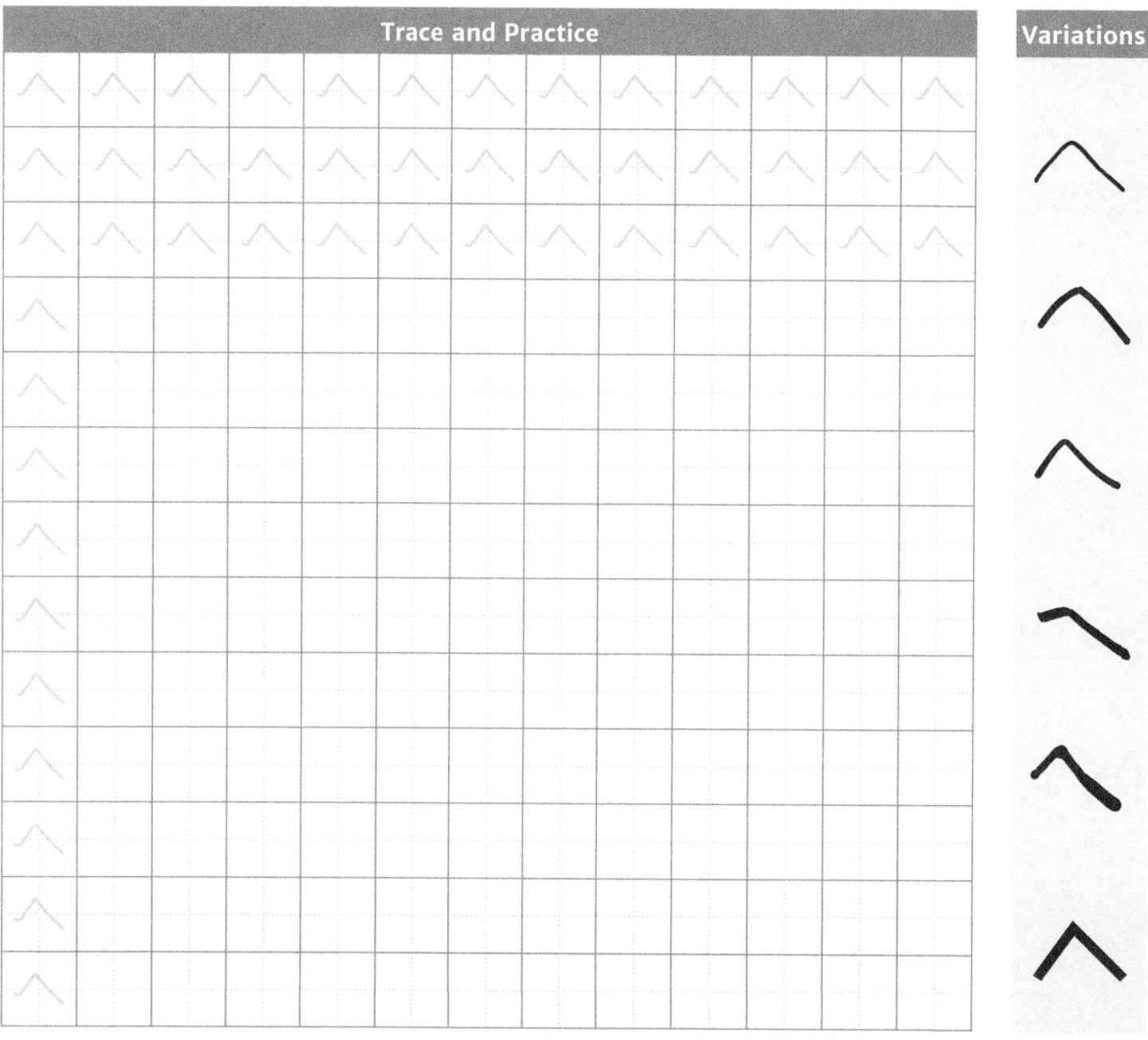

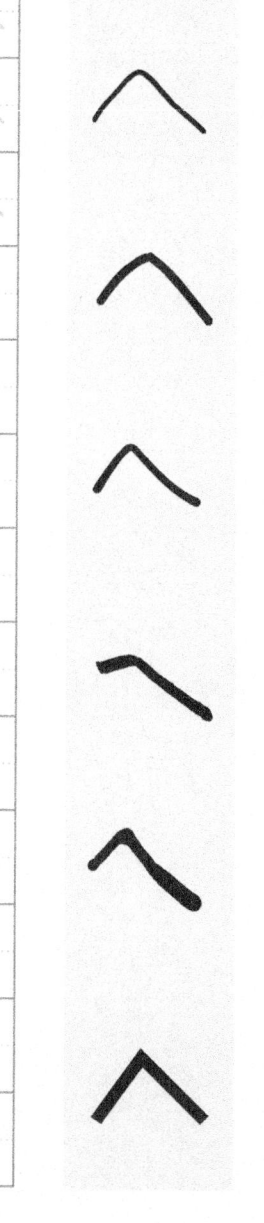

Example Word

ヘルニア

Herunia

Translation: Hernia

Trace and Practice

Variations

82

Stroke Order

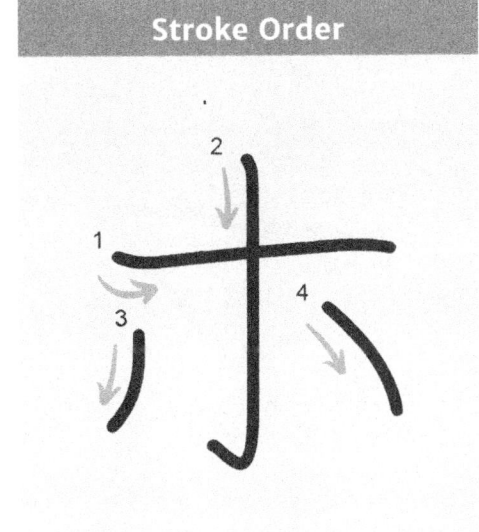

Stroke Progression

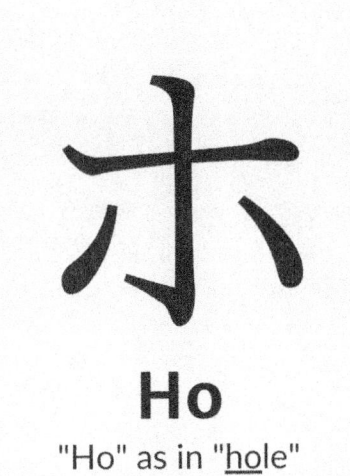

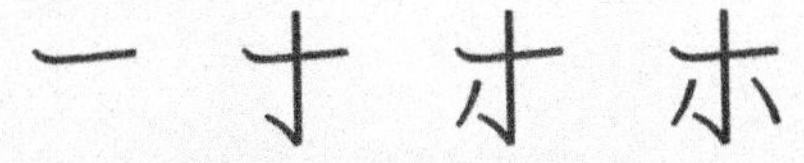

一 ナ オ ホ

Example Word

ホワイト

Howaito

Translation: White

Ho

"Ho" as in "hole"

IPA: /ho/

Trace and Practice

Variations

ホ ホ ホ ホ ホ ホ

Ma
"Ma" as in the name "Mark"
IPA: /ma/

Stroke Order

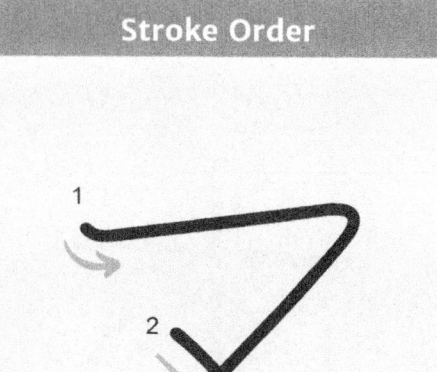

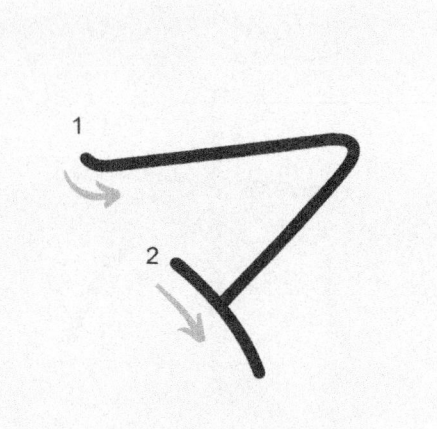

Stroke Progression
フ マ

Example Word
マフィン
Mafin
Translation: Muffin

Trace and Practice

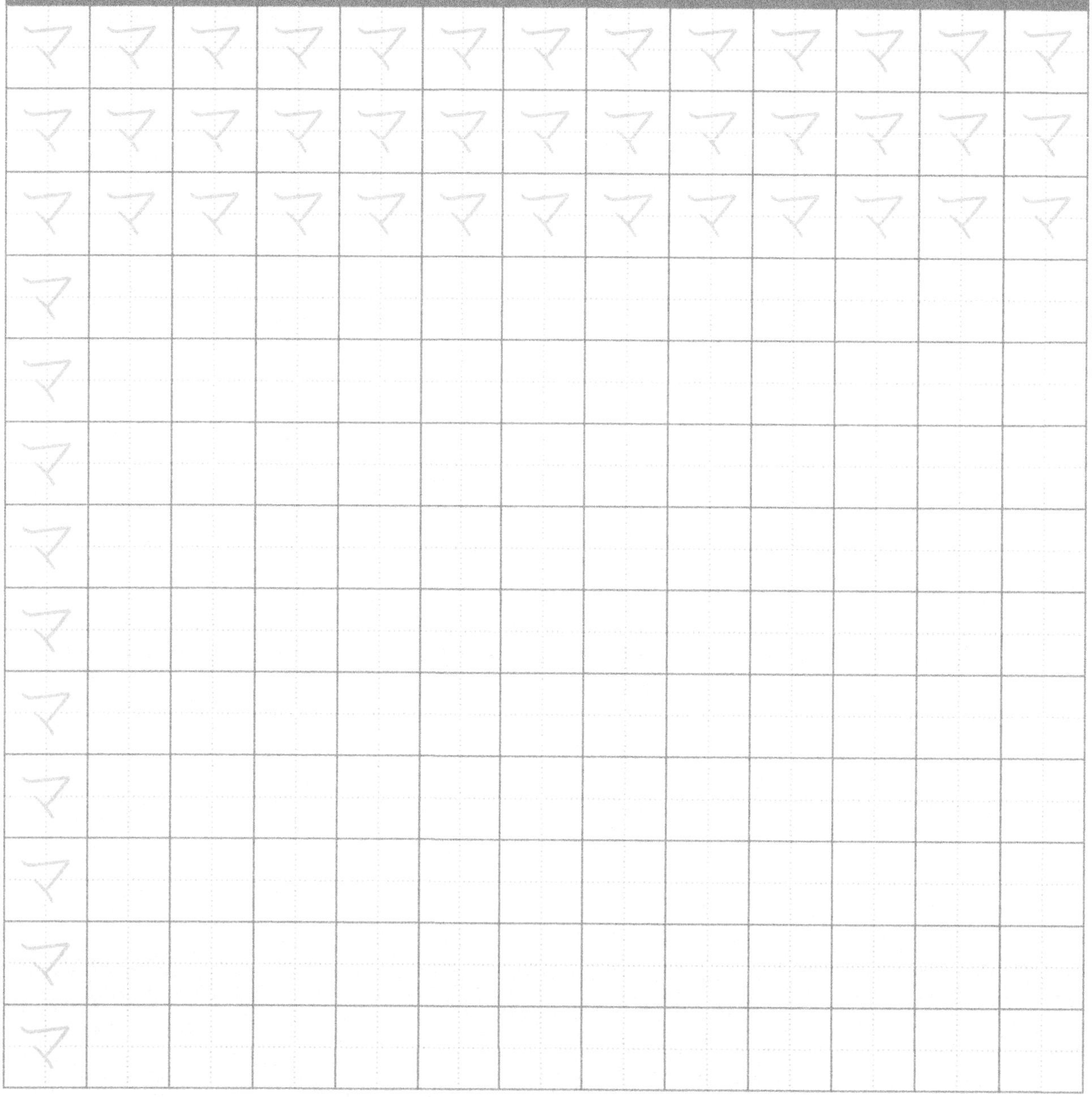

Variations

Mi

"Mi" as in "milk"

IPA: /mi/

Stroke Order

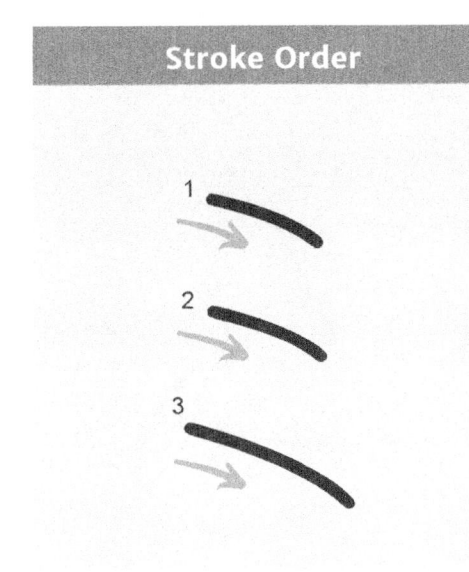

1
2
3

Stroke Progression

Example Word

ミキサー

Mikisā

Translation: Blender / Mixer

Trace and Practice

Variations

Stroke Order

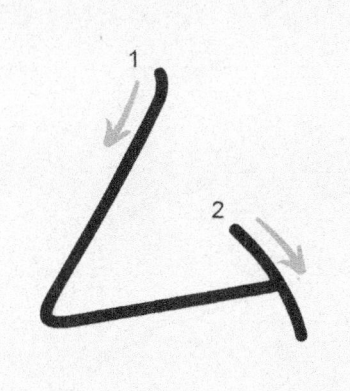

Stroke Progression

ム

Example Word

ムービー

Mūbī

Translation: Movie

Mu

"Moo" as in "Moon"

IPA: /mɯ/

Trace and Practice

Variations

86

Me
"Me" as in "Met"
IPA: /me/

Stroke Order

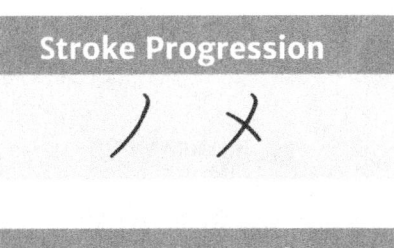

Stroke Progression
ノ メ

Example Word
メモリー

Memorī

Translation: Memory

Trace and Practice

Variations

Mo

Similar to "ko" as in "Korea"

IPA: /ko/

Stroke Order

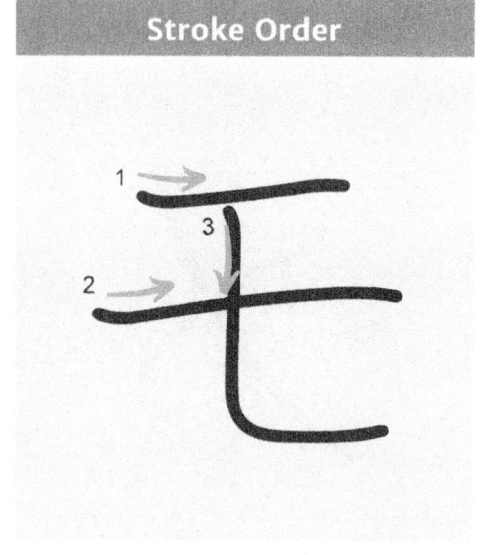

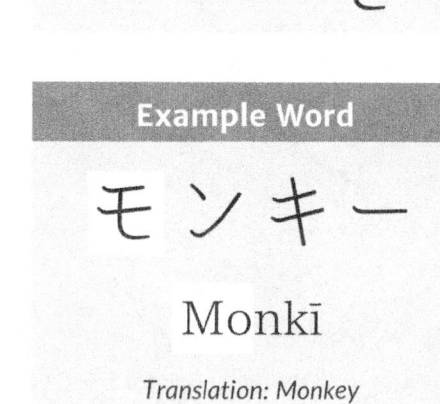

Stroke Progression
一 二 モ

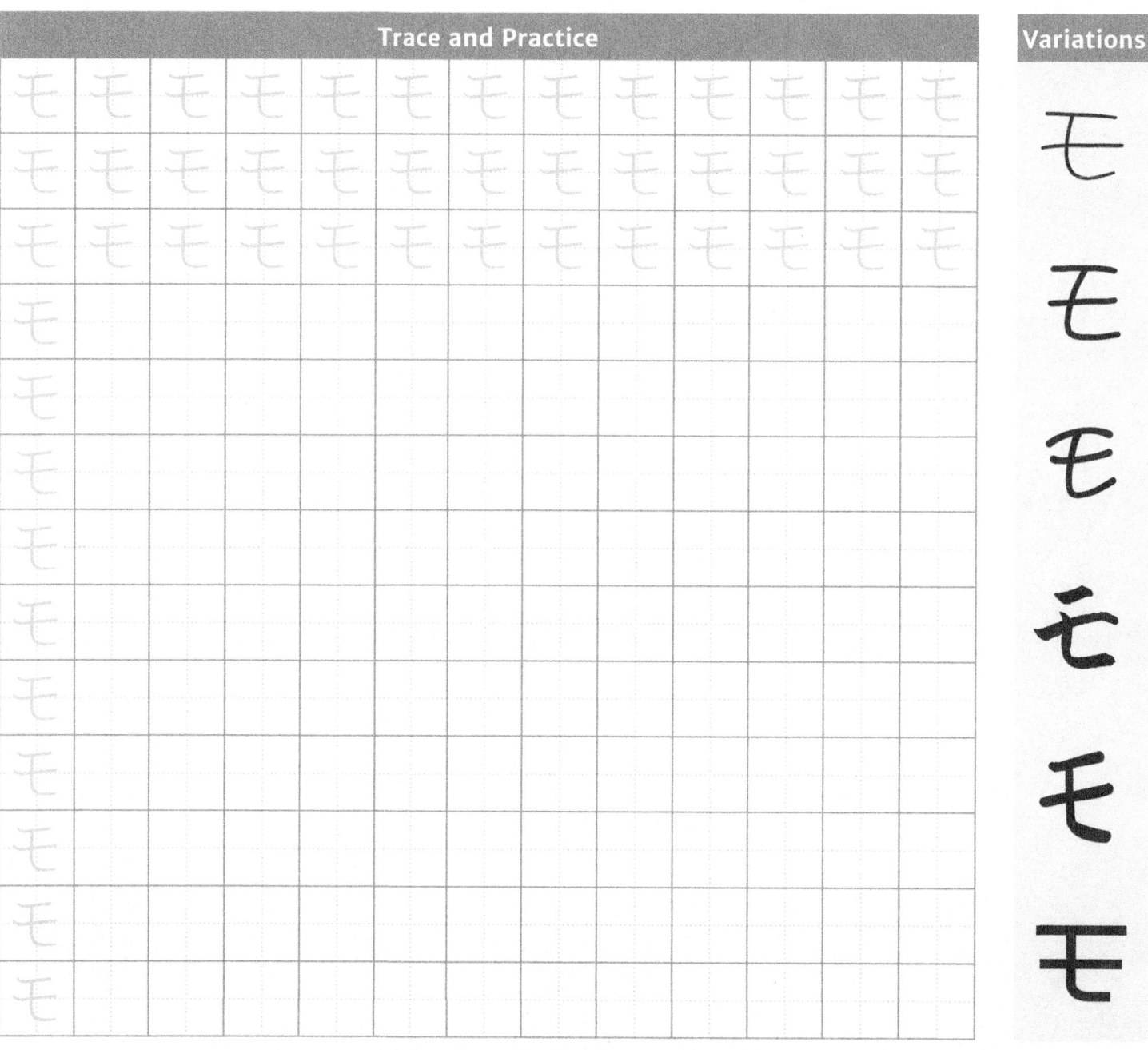

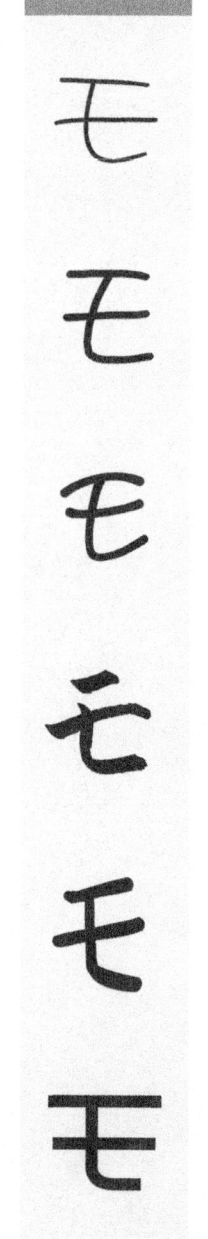

Example Word
モンキー

Monkī

Translation: Monkey

Trace and Practice

Variations

Ya

"Ya" as in "yacht"

IPA: /ja/

Stroke Order

Stroke Progression

⁻ ヤ

Example Word

ヤマネコ

Yamaneko

Translation: Wildcar

Trace and Practice

Variations

Yu

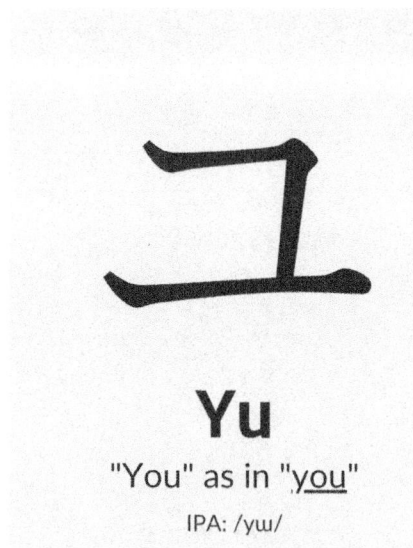

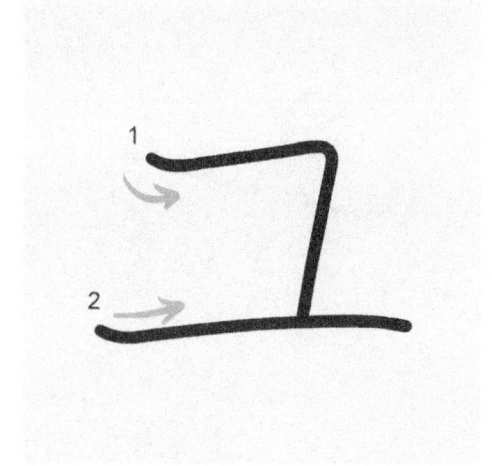

"You" as in "you"

IPA: /yɯ/

Stroke Order

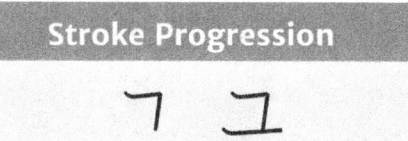

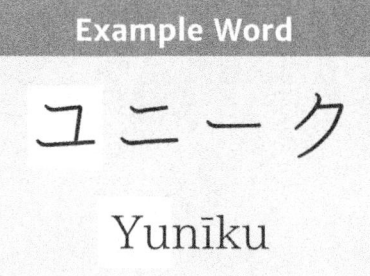

Stroke Progression

Example Word

ユニーク

Yunīku

Translation: Unique

Trace and Practice

Variations

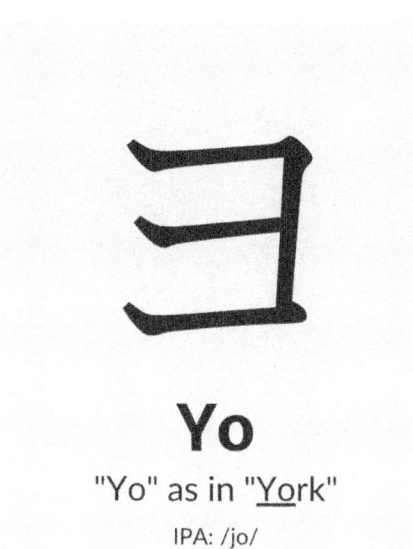

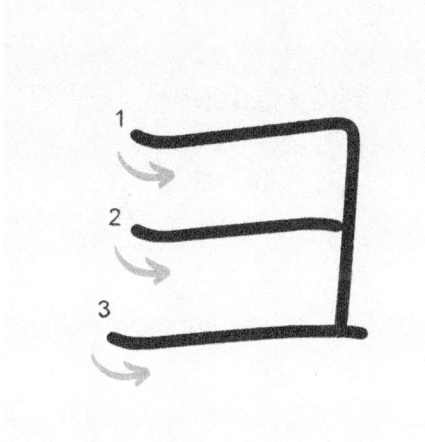

Stroke Order

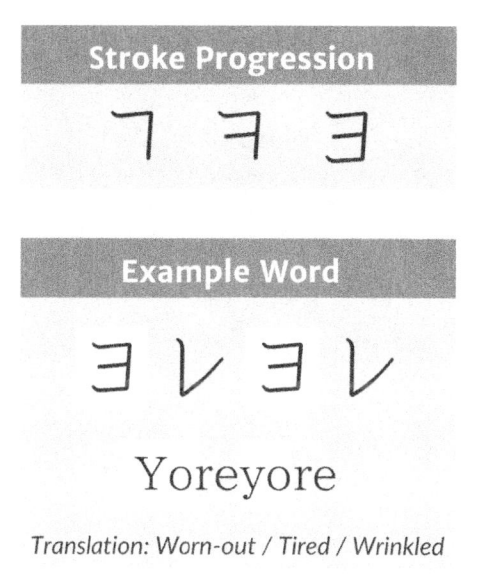

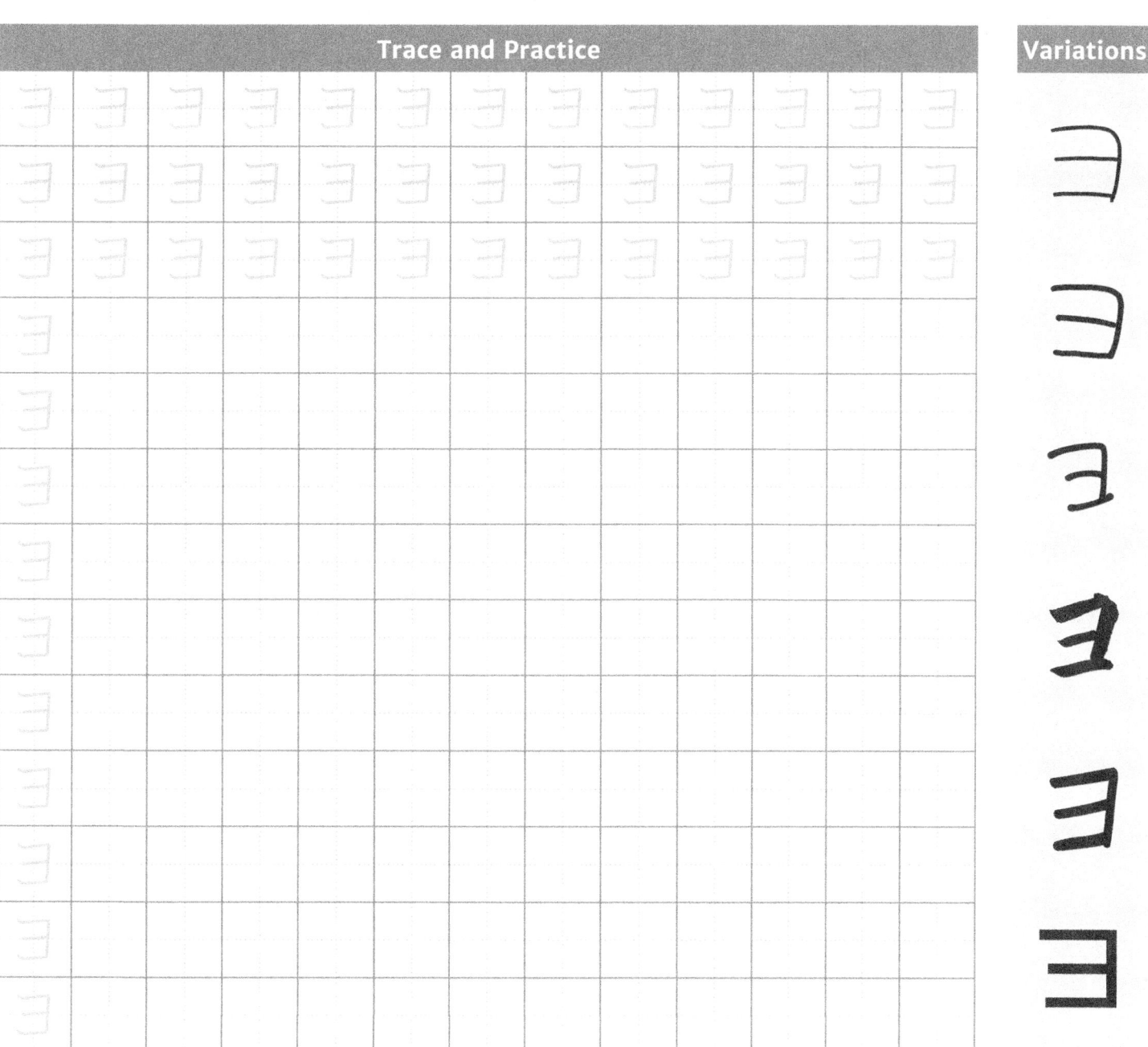

Stroke Progression

ア ㋐ ヨ

Example Word

ヨレヨレ

Yoreyore

Translation: Worn-out / Tired / Wrinkled

Yo
"Yo" as in "York"

IPA: /jo/

Trace and Practice

Variations

Stroke Order

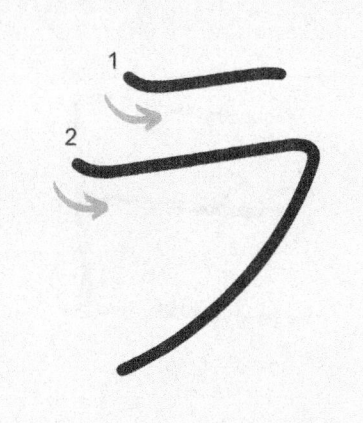

Stroke Progression

Example Word

ラグーン

Ragūn

Translation: Lagoon

Ra

"Ra" with a rolled "r" as in the Italian word "ragazzi"

IPA: /ra/

Trace and Practice

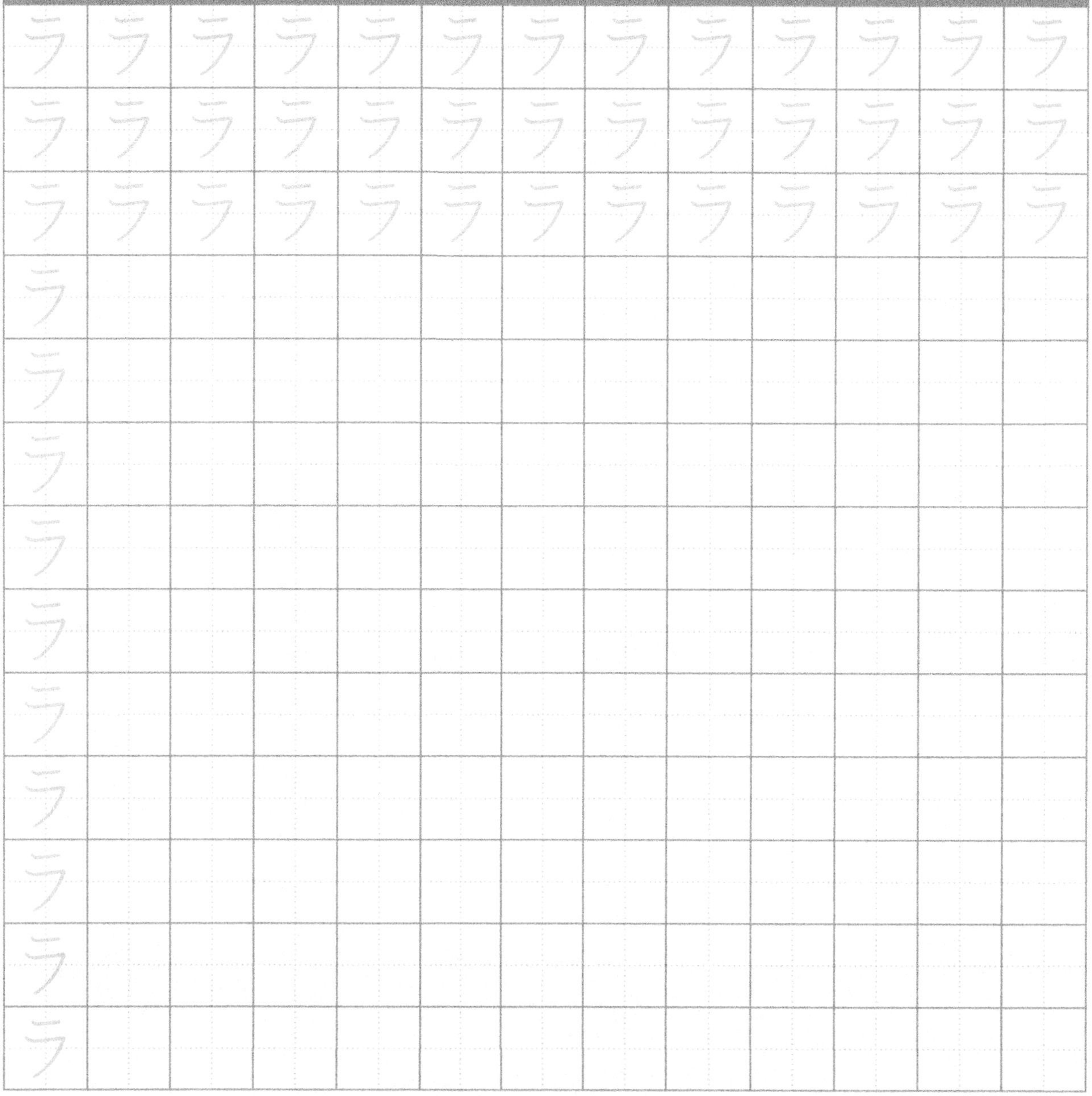

Variations

92

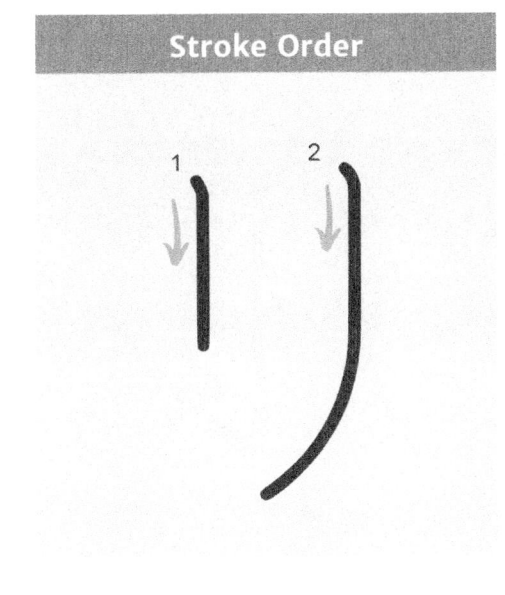

Stroke Order

Stroke Progression
ㇴ リ

Example Word
リセット

Risetto

Translation: Reset

リ
Chi

Rolled "r" as in the Italian word "ragazzi" pronounced together with an "i" as in "Italy"

IPA: /ri/

Trace and Practice

Variations

93

ル

Ru

Rolled "r" as in the Italian word "ragazzi" pronounced together with an "Oo" as in "zoo"

IPA: /ɾɯ/

Stroke Order

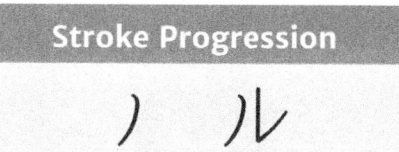

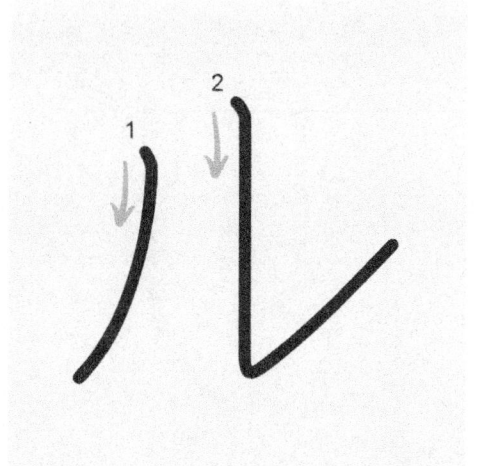

Stroke Progression

ノ ル

Example Word

ルーター

Rūtā

Translation: Router

Trace and Practice

Variations

レ

Re

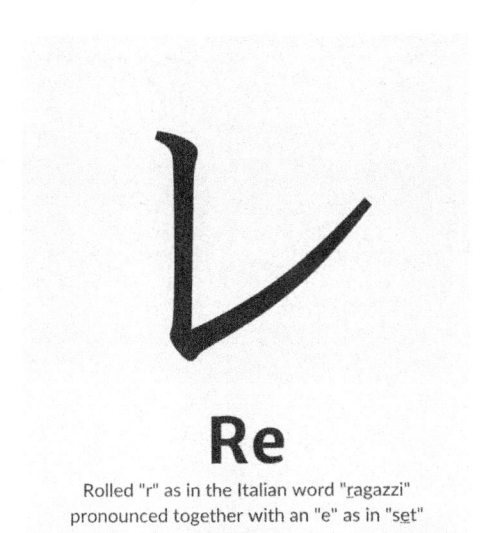

Rolled "r" as in the Italian word "ragazzi" pronounced together with an "e" as in "set"

IPA: /re/

Stroke Order

Stroke Progression

レ

Example Word

レディー

Redī

Translation: Ready

Trace and Practice

Variations

Ro

Rolled "r" as in the Italian word "ragazzi" pronounced together with an "o" as in "boat"

IPA: /ro/

Stroke Order

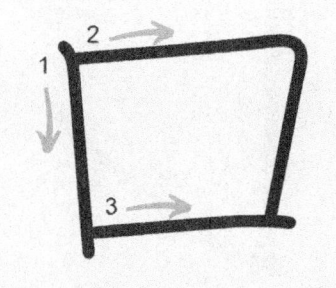

Stroke Progression

Example Word

ログイン

Roguin

Translation: Login

Trace and Practice

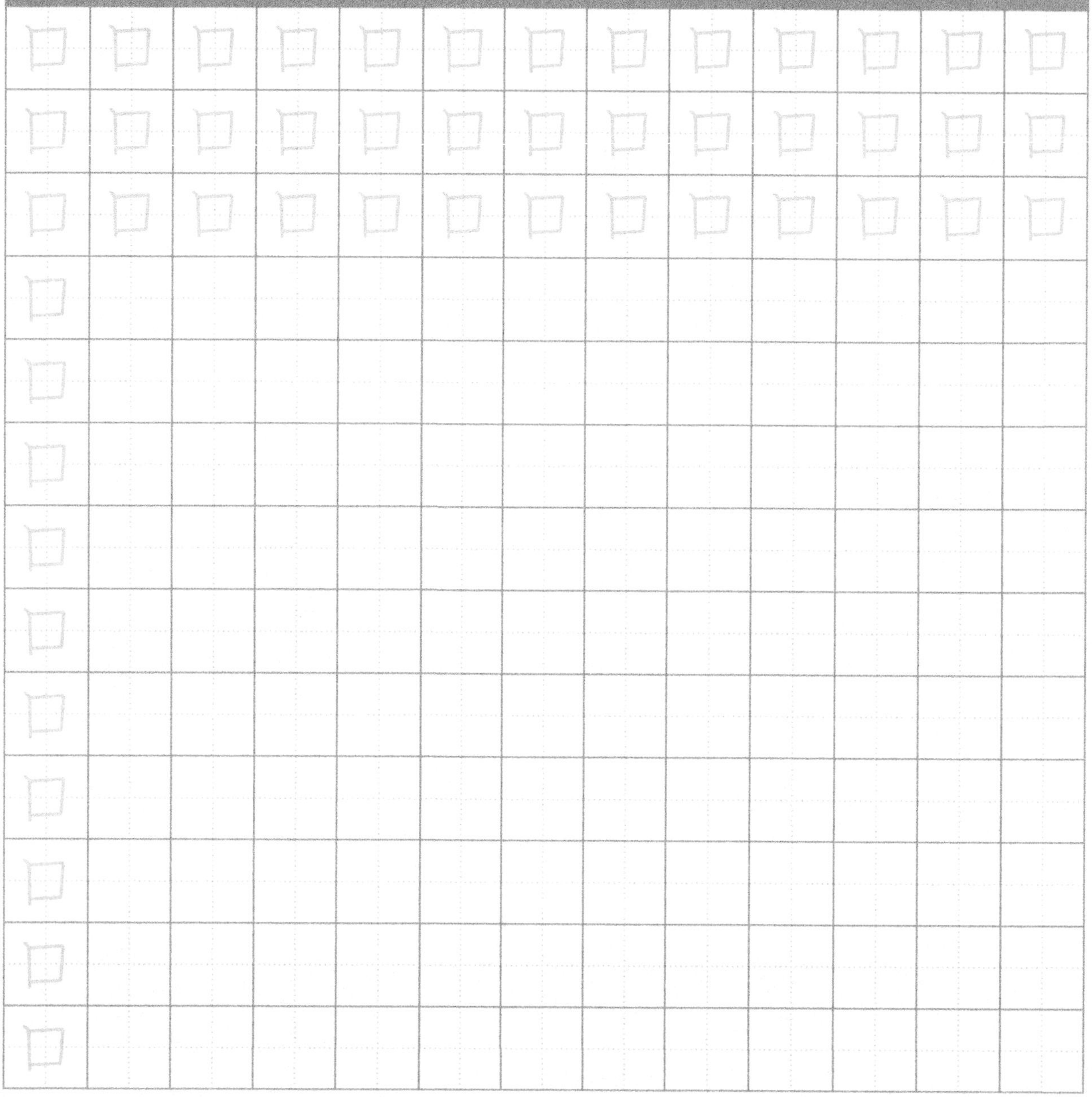

Variations

Wa

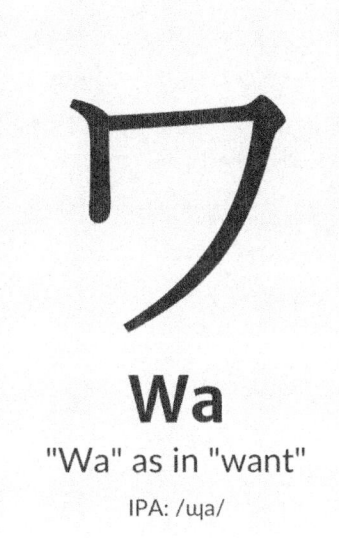

ワ

"Wa" as in "want"

IPA: /ɰa/

Stroke Order

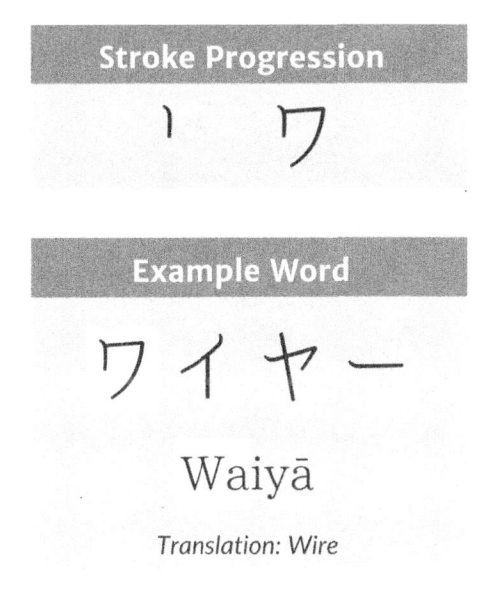

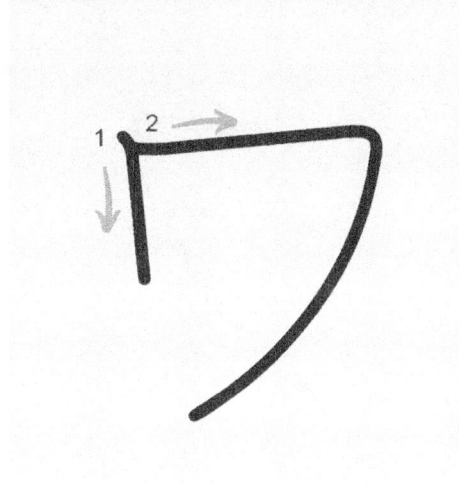

Stroke Progression
丶 ワ

Example Word
ワイヤー

Waiyā

Translation: Wire

Trace and Practice

Variations

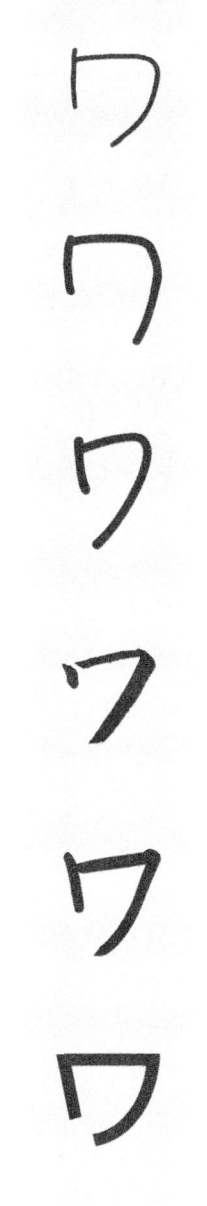

Wo
"O" as in "b**o**at"
IPA: /o/

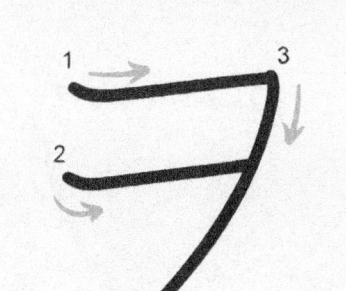

Stroke Order

Stroke Progression

Example Word

The katakana character "ヲ" is used almost exclusively for stylistic reasons.

Example: When robots speak in Japanese Manga their speech is often written using the katakana syllabary instead of the hiragana characters. In instances like this, the particle "を" will exceptionally be represented as "ヲ".

Trace and Practice

Variations

ン

N

"N" as in "not"

IPA: /n/, /m/, /ɲ/, /ŋ/ or /ɯ̃]

Stroke Order

1, 2

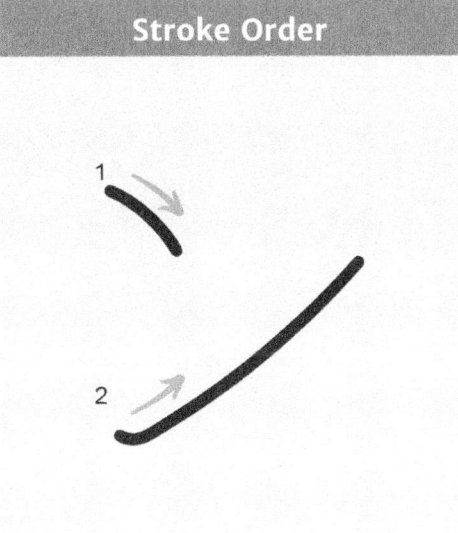

Stroke Progression

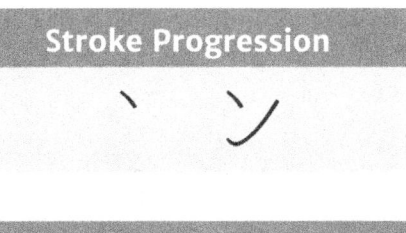

丶 ン

Example Word

デザイン

Dezain

Translation: Design

Trace and Practice

Variations

Sokuon

ッ

The syllable immediately after ッ is duplicated but its vowel sound is removed. Effectively, this means doubling the consonant sound without doubling the vowel sound. At the end of a word in represents a glottal stop.

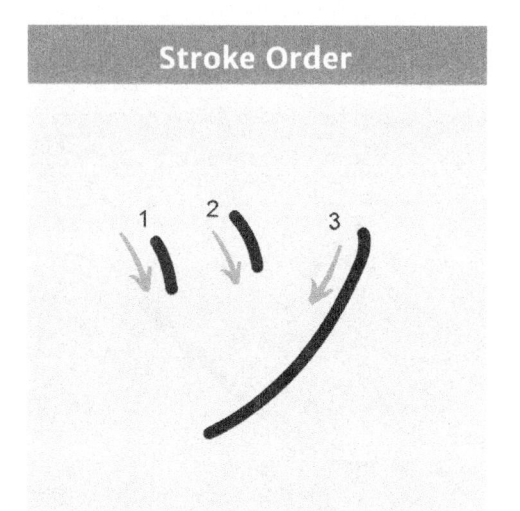

Stroke Order

Stroke Progression

ヽ　ヾ　ッ

Example Word

アップル

Appuru

Translation: Apple

Trace and Practice

Variations

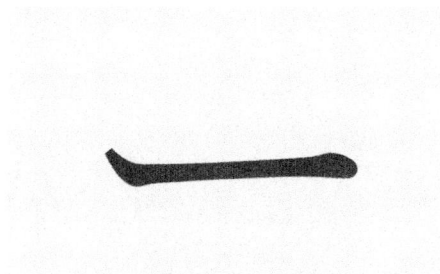

Chōonpu

Commonly used in katakana and more rarely in hiragana, the chōonpu, also known as the Katakana-Hiragana Prolonged Sound Mark, indicates that the preceding vowel should be pronounced as a long vowel. This can be transliterated by either doubling the vowel (example: "aa") or by adding a "-" sign on top of the long vowel (example "ā").

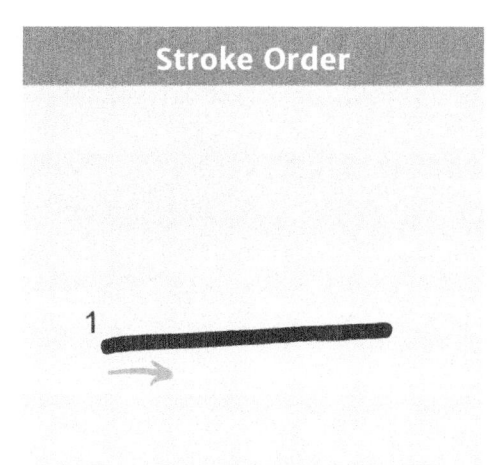

Stroke Order

1 →

Stroke Progression

Example Word

イタリー

Itarī / Itarii

Translation: Italy

Trace and Practice

Variations

Bonus Training Page — Photocopy Me Freely

Bonus Training Page – Photocopy Me Freely

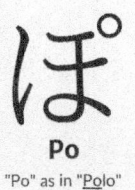

Hiragana Diacritics Reference Chart: The Dakuten and the Handakuten

Now that you have mastered all the hiragana and katakana characters in current use, you are ready to learn about the **dakuten** and the **handakuten**.

The dakuten and the handakuten are two very special diacritical marks. With them, you can produce 25 new syllabic sounds. Since you already know how to handwrite each of the base characters, in the following pages you'll learn to trace both the dakuten and the handakuten and you'll have acess to 2 complete reference charts. One for the hiragana syllabary and another for the katakana characters.

Dakuten
Voicing Mark
The dakuten is drawn last, as a single stroke, after having drawn all the strokes of the main character.

Handakuten
Half Voicing Mark
The handakuten strokes are also drawn after the main character, from the left to the right.

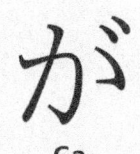

が	ぎ	ぐ	げ	ご
Ga	**Gi**	**Gu**	**Ge**	**Go**
"Ga" as in "Gallon"	"Gi" as in "Give"	"Gu" as in "Guardia"	"Ge" as in "Get"	"Go" as in "Go"
IPA: /ga/	IPA: /gi/	IPA: /gɯ/	IPA: /ge/	IPA: /go/

ざ	じ	ず	ぜ	ぞ
Za	**ji**	**Zu**	**Ze**	**Zo**
"Za" as in "Zaire"	"Ge" as in "Genius"	"Zoo" as in "Zoo"	"Ze" as in "Zest"	"Zo" as in "Zone"
IPA: /(d)za/	IPA: /(d)zi/	IPA: /(d)zɯ/	IPA: /(d)ze/	IPA: /(d)zo/

だ	ぢ	づ	で	ど
Da	**Ji / Dji / Jyi**	**Dzu / Zu**	**De**	**Do**
"Da" as in "Dalmatian"	"Ge" as in "Genius"	A "D" sound followed by "Zoo" as in "Zoo"	"De" as in "Dennis"	"Do" as in "Dough"
IPA: /da/	IPA: /(d)zi/	IPA: /(d)zɯ/	IPA: /de/	IPA: /do/

ば	び	ぶ	べ	ぼ
Ba	**Bi**	**Bu**	**Be**	**Bo**
"Ba" as in "Balm"	"Bi" as in "Big"	"Bu" as in "Bull"	"Be" as in "Beg"	"Bo" as in "Boat"
IPA: /ba/	IPA: /bi/	IPA: /bɯ/	IPA: /be/	IPA: /bo/

ぱ	ぴ	ぷ	ぺ	ぽ
Pa	**Pi**	**Pu**	**Pe**	**Po**
"Pa" as in "Palm Tree"	"Pi" as in "Pig"	"Poo" as in "Pool"	"Pe" as in "Peck"	"Po" as in "Polo"
IPA: /ga/	IPA: /pa/	IPA: /pɯ/	IPA: /pe/	IPA: /po/

Katakana Diacritics Reference Chart: The Dakuten and the Handakuten

The **dakuten** is known as the "ten-ten," a Japanese expression meaning "dots."

The **handuken**, on the other hand, is known as the "maru," an expression meaning "circle."

Remembering this will make it easier to recall which one is which.

Dakuten
Voicing Mark
The dakuten is drawn last, as a single stroke, after having drawn all the strokes of the main character.

Handakuten
Half Voicing Mark
The handakuten strokes are also drawn after the main character, from the left to the right.

ガ
Ga
"Ga" as in "Gallon"
IPA: /ga/

ギ
Gi
"Gi" as in "Give"
IPA: /gi/

グ
Gu
"Gu" as in "Guardia"
IPA: /gɯ/

ゲ
Ge
"Ge" as in "Get"
IPA: /ge/

ゴ
Go
"Go" as in "Go"
IPA: /go/

ザ
Za
"Za" as in "Zaire"
IPA: /(d)za/

ジ
ji
"Ge" as in "Genius"
IPA: /(d)ʑi/

ズ
Zu
"Zoo" as in "Zoo"
IPA: /(d)zɯ/

ゼ
Ze
"Ze" as in "Zest"
IPA: /(d)ze/

ゾ
Zo
"Zo" as in "Zone"
IPA: /(d)zo/

ダ
Da
"Da" as in "Dalmatian"
IPA: /da/

ヂ
Ji / Dji / Jyi
"Ge" as in "Genius"
IPA: /(d)ʑi/

ヅ
Dzu / Zu
A "D" sound followed by "Zoo" as in "Zoo"
IPA: /(d)zɯ/

デ
De
"De" as in "Dennis"
IPA: /de/

ド
Do
"Do" as in "Dough"
IPA: /do/

バ
Ba
"Ba" as in "Balm"
IPA: /ba/

ビ
Bi
"Bi" as in "Big"
IPA: /bi/

ブ
Bu
"Bu" as in "Bull"
IPA: /bɯ/

ベ
Be
"Be" as in "Beg"
IPA: /be/

ボ
Bo
"Bo" as in "Boat"
IPA: /bo/

パ
Pa
"Pa" as in "Palm Tree"
IPA: /ga/

ピ
Pi
"Pi" as in "Pig"
IPA: /pa/

プ
Pu
"Poo" as in "Pool"
IPA: /pɯ/

ペ
Pe
"Pe" as in "Peck"
IPA: /pe/

ポ
Po
"Po" as in "Polo"
IPA: /po/

Hiragana Reference Chart: The Yōon Digraphs

In Japanese there are 7 hiragana syllables ending in "i". These are: き (Ki), し (Shi), ち (Chi), に (Ni), ひ (Hi), み (Mi), and り (Ri). We'll call these our "**7i**" syllables, for short.

Then, you also have 3 syllables that start with "y." These are: や (Ya), ゆ (Yu), and よ (Yo). We'll call these our "**3y**" syllables.

When any of the **7i** syllables is followed by any of the **3y** syllables one of two things can happen: (1) They can either be forming a single combined sound, called a diphthong, or (2) they can just be representing 2 separate syllables like you'd expect.

How can you tell the difference?

In the past you'd need to rely on context and in a good understanding of the Japanese language. Nowadays, however, things are much easier.

Whenever the **3y** are forming the special combined sound with the previous 7i syllable, they'll be drawn smaller than the surrounding characters.

This special combination is called a yōon 拗音 (ようおん). In simple terms it means that two different syllables will be forming a single sound instead of the expected two.

Example word that illustrates this difference:

きょげん　きよい
Kyogen　Kiyoi

In the case of きょげん (translation: lie), the よ syllable is clearly smaller than the surrounding characters. This makes it clear that the preceding syllable (き) should be combined with よ to form a single "kyo" sound. In the case of きよい (translation: pure, clear, platonic) a full sized よ indicates きよ should be pronounced as "ki" + "yo" or "kiyo" instead of "kyo".

きゃ **Kya** IPA: /kʲa/	きゅ **Kyu** IPA: /kʲɯ/	きょ **Kyo** IPA: /kʲo/
しゃ **Sha** IPA: /ɕa/	しゅ **Shu** IPA: /ɕɯ/	しょ **Sho** IPA: /ɕo/
ちゃ **Cha** IPA: /tɕa/	ちゅ **Chu** IPA: /tɕɯ/	ちょ **Cho** IPA: /tɕo/
にゃ **Nya** IPA: /ɲa/	にゅ **Nyu** IPA: /ɲɯ/	にょ **Nyo** IPA: /ɲo/
ひゃ **Hya** IPA: /ça/	ひゅ **Hyu** IPA: /çɯ/	ひょ **Hyo** IPA: /ço/
みゃ **Mya** IPA: /mʲa/	みゅ **Myu** IPA: /mʲɯ/	みょ **Myo** IPA: /mʲo/
りゃ **Rya** IPA: /ɾʲa/	りゅ **Ryu** IPA: /ɾʲɯ/	りょ **Ryo** IPA: /ɾʲo/

Katakana Reference Chart: The Yōon Digraphs

In Japanese there are also 7 katakana syllables ending in "i". These are: キ (Ki), シ (Shi), チ (Chi), ニ (Ni), ヒ (Hi), ミ (Mi), and リ (Ri).

Then, you also have 3 syllables that start with "y." These are: ヤ (Ya), ユ (Yu), and ヨ (Yo).

Like in hiragana, they'll be drawn smaller than the surrounding characters whenever they are forming a single combined sound with the previous character.

A closer look at the difference in size across multiple fonts:

Hiragana	やゃ	やゃ	やゃ	やゃ	やゃ	やゃ	やゃ	やゃ
	ゆゅ	ゆゅ	ゆゅ	ゆゅ	ゆゅ	ゆゅ	ゆゅ	ゆゅ
	よょ	よょ	よょ	よょ	よょ	よょ	よょ	よょ
Katakana	ヤャ	ヤャ	ヤャ	ヤャ	ヤャ	ヤャ	ヤャ	ヤャ
	ユュ	ユュ	ユュ	ユュ	ユュ	ユュ	ユュ	ユュ
	ヨョ	ヨョ	ヨョ	ヨョ	ヨョ	ヨョ	ヨョ	ヨョ

キャ **Kya** IPA: /kʲa/
キュ **Kyu** IPA: /kʲɯ/
キョ **Kyo** IPA: /kʲo/

シャ **Sha** IPA: /ɕa/
シュ **Shu** IPA: /ɕɯ/
ショ **Sho** IPA: /ɕo/

チャ **Cha** IPA: /tɕa/
チュ **Chu** IPA: /tɕɯ/
チョ **Cho** IPA: /tɕo/

ニャ **Nya** IPA: /ɲa/
ニュ **Nyu** IPA: /ɲɯ/
ニョ **Nyo** IPA: /ɲo/

ヒャ **Hya** IPA: /ça/
ヒュ **Hyu** IPA: /çɯ/
ヒョ **Hyo** IPA: /ço/

ミャ **Mya** IPA: /mʲa/
ミュ **Myu** IPA: /mʲɯ/
ミョ **Myo** IPA: /mʲo/

リャ **Rya** IPA: /rʲa/
リュ **Ryu** IPA: /rʲɯ/
リョ **Ryo** IPA: /rʲo/

Reference Chart: Combining the Yōon Digraphs With the Dakuten and the Handakuten

Hiragana

ぎゃ **Gya** IPA: /gʲa/	ぎゅ **Gyu** IPA: /gʲɯ/	ぎょ **Gyo** IPA: /gʲo/
じゃ **Ja** IPA: /(d)ʑa/	じゅ **Ju** IPA: /(d)ʑɯ/	じょ **Jo** IPA: /(d)ʑo/
ぢゃ **Ja** IPA: /(d)ʑa/	ぢゅ **Ju** IPA: /(d)ʑɯ/	ぢょ **Jo** IPA: /(d)ʑo/
びゃ **Bya** IPA: /bʲa/	びゅ **Byu** IPA: /bʲɯ/	びょ **Byo** IPA: /bʲo/
ぴゃ **Pya** IPA: /pʲa/	ぴゅ **Pyu** IPA: /pʲɯ/	ぴょ **Pyo** IPA: /pʲo/

Katakana

ギャ **Gya** IPA: /gʲa/	ギュ **Gyu** IPA: /gʲɯ/	ギョ **Gyo** IPA: /gʲo/
ジャ **Ja** IPA: /(d)ʑa/	ジュ **Ju** IPA: /(d)ʑɯ/	ジョ **Jo** IPA: /(d)ʑo/
ヂャ **Ja** IPA: /(d)ʑa/	ヂュ **Ju** IPA: /(d)ʑɯ/	ヂョ **Jo** IPA: /(d)ʑo/
ビャ **Bya** IPA: /bʲa/	ビュ **Byu** IPA: /bʲɯ/	ビョ **Byo** IPA: /bʲo/
ピャ **Pya** IPA: /pʲa/	ピュ **Pyu** IPA: /pʲɯ/	ピョ **Pyo** IPA: /pʲo/

Bonus Training Page — Photocopy Me Freely

Bonus Training Page – Photocopy Me Freely

Bonus Training Page — Photocopy Me Freely

Bonus Training Page – Photocopy Me Freely

Bonus Training Page – Photocopy Me Freely

Bonus Training Page – Photocopy Me Freely

Bonus Training Page – Photocopy Me Freely

Bonus Training Page – Photocopy Me Freely

Printed in Great Britain
by Amazon